10605490

Astro Herbalism

North American edition published by
Timber Press 2026

Timber Press
Workman Publishing
Hachette Book Group, Inc.
1290 Avenue of the Americas
New York, New York 10104
timberpress.com

Timber Press is an imprint of Workman Publishing, a division of Hachette Book Group, Inc. The Timber Press name and logo are registered trademarks of Hachette Book Group, Inc.

Printed in China by 1010 International Printing Ltd on responsibly sourced paper.

Conceived, edited, and designed by
Quarto Publishing, an imprint of
The Quarto Group, 1 Triptych Place, London SE1 9SH
Original design and art direction: Hello Daly
Design: Karin Skånberg
Designer: Eliana Holder

ISBN 978-1-64326-554-4

A catalog record for this book is available from the Library of Congress.

CAUTION
This book is not intended as a substitute for the advice of a health care professional. Always seek professional advice before using any treatment, and stop treatment immediately if you feel worse or suffer any adverse reaction. The author, publisher, and copyright holders assume no responsibility for any injury or damage caused or sustained by any person acting or refraining from acting as a result of reliance on the material in this publication.

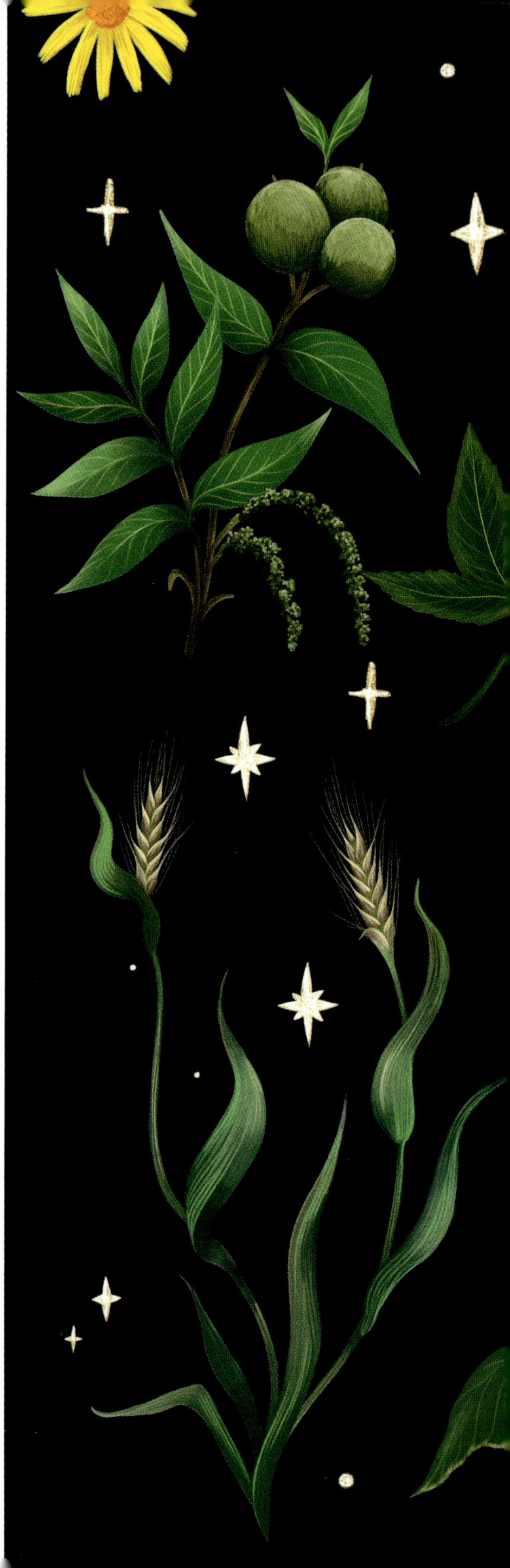

Astro Herbalism

Holistic Wellness and Self-Discovery through Herbalism and Astrology

Jessica Rosset
Illustrated by Anna Stead

Contents

Meet Jessica

At the age of 12, I found a book left behind by a stranger at my auntie's coffee shop. A total booklover, I asked if I could read it until the owner returned to claim it. Sun Signs *by Linda Goodman was never retrieved, and I am forever grateful to that stranger for opening the door to astrology, which became a strong foundation for my work and personality from that moment.*

My path later led me to study psychology, driven by a fascination with mythology, archetypes, and the mysteries of the unconscious. I completed my clinical training in psychodynamic therapy and Jungian practice, deepening my understanding of the connections between psyche, symbolism, and transformation. Influenced by thinkers such as Carl Jung, Joseph Campbell, Marion Woodman, Clarissa Pinkola Estés, and James Hillman, my work is grounded in both depth psychology and the exploration of myth, consciousness, and the transcendental realm.

My interest in herbalism emerged in my late twenties, initiated by a personal need. Struggling with severe PMS symptoms and unwilling to rely on pharmaceutical antidepressants, I turned to plants for healing. My research led me to discover the powerful benefits of the chaste tree (Vitex agnus- castus), an herb traditionally used to support hormonal balance. Suddenly, I felt that, with that plant, my whole life had changed. The experience opened my eyes to the magical relationship between plants and the human body, a relationship not just physical, but spiritual.

From there, my exploration expanded into herbal studies, eventually leading me to combine my passions for astrology and plant medicine. I began crafting astrological perfumes, blending plant energies and astrological principles into wearable scents. My work naturally evolved into teaching, and now I guide others in understanding the deep correspondences between the planets of our Solar System and the plants around us.

Today, I work as a psychotherapist, astrologer, and teacher. Alongside writing and teaching about astrology, herbalism, and Jungian psychology, I offer private therapy sessions, astrology consultations, and Astro Herbalism sessions. I invite those who encounter my work, including you, the reader of this book, to remember that you are part of a larger story, one that talks about the soul, the body, and the living world around you.

What is *Astro Herbalism?*

Astrology and herbalism are two ancient ways of knowing, two living traditions that help us understand ourselves and the world around us. When you bring them together, something powerful happens: you start to see yourself and the plants around you as part of a larger, interconnected cosmos.

Astrology maps the soul's landscape; it reveals the forces that shape our strengths, our struggles, and our growth. Herbalism connects us back to the living Earth; it reminds us that healing is not mechanical—it is alive and rooted in nature's intelligence.

Astro Herbalism explores how the energies of the planets and the properties of medicinal plants mirror one another. You'll see how the planetary movements across the sky are reflected not only in human life, but also in the medicine the Earth offers us. The plants are not random; the planets are not distant. They speak to each other, and to you.

As Above, So Below

At the heart of this path is a simple but profound truth: we are not separate from the cosmos; we are participants in its unfolding. The same forces that pull the tides also shape the inner currents of our emotions. The same patterns that trace the orbit of Saturn also show up in the patterns of aging, maturity, and resilience within our bodies.

Ancient cultures understood this. In ancient Greece, astrology was not separate from philosophy or medicine; instead, it was part of a unified vision of life. Physicians used astrology to diagnose and treat illnesses and the philosopher Plato spoke of the "Music of the Spheres"—the idea, based on Pythagoras' (c.570–c.490 BC) theories, that the Universe was underpinned by logical, mathematical principles, in much the same way as music. In the ancient civilizations of Egypt, India, China, and elsewhere, the stars were seen as guides for spiritual growth and physical healing, and healers worked with the stars as part of medicine. In these societies, astrology was studied alongside botany, alchemy, and natural philosophy. Physicians such as Hippocrates (c.460–c.375 BC) believed that the body could not be treated without also considering the heavens. Herbs were prescribed based not only on physical symptoms but also on a person's constitution, temperament, and astrological charts.

Today, many of us have lost that sense of connection. Technology moves faster than the human soul. And as a result, many of us now find ourselves feeling rootless, overwhelmed, alienated from nature, and even from our own bodies.

Understanding Astrological Principles in Herbalism

At the core of Celestial Herbalism is the principle of correspondence: the idea that everything in the Universe reflects everything else. The energies of the planets are not just "out there"—they live inside plants, inside the human body, and inside every cycle of growth and decay. Each celestial body, from the Sun to the distant dwarf planet Pluto, has an archetypal force. That force plays out through astrological signs, planetary aspects, and house placements, creating a complex but meaningful pattern of influence on both individuals and the collective as a whole.

Plants, too, carry energetic signatures. They are not just biochemical substances; they are also expressions of specific cosmic qualities.

Herbalists have long noticed how certain plants align with particular planetary forces. For example, solar herbs, such as St. John's wort and calendula, carry the brightness and vitality of the Sun. They strengthen the immune system, lift the mood, and restore a sense of wholeness and confidence. Saturnian herbs, such as common comfrey and mullein, are another good example. They reflect the grounding, structuring, and boundary-making qualities of Saturn. They help to rebuild tissue, support bone health, and promote emotional endurance during times of hardship.

These patterns are not random; they arise from a deep resonance between the life force of the plant and the life force of the cosmos.

By understanding the astrological correspondences of herbs, you will gain a more intuitive and precise way to work with plant medicine. You can choose herbs, not just based on symptoms, but also on the underlying energetic imbalances that symptoms reflect. For example, if someone struggles with

boundaries and emotional depletion (common signs of an underactive Saturn), you might reach for Saturnian plants to build resilience and containment, rather than only treating surface symptoms such as fatigue or anxiety. Or if someone feels disconnected, lost, or lacking in purpose (an imbalanced relationship with the Sun), you might work with solar plants to reignite their inner light.

Start With Your Astrological Birth Chart

To work with Astro Herbalism personally, it helps to know your astrological birth chart, which is a map of where the planets were at the exact time and place you were born.

If you don't already have your birth chart, you can have an astrologer cast and interpret it for you, or you can generate it online yourself. There are many options available, but I recommend websites like Astro.com, Horoscopes.astro-seek.com, or costarastrology.com for accurate charts and interpretations. Once you have your chart in front of you, focus first on a few key elements:

- Your **Sun sign** (core vitality)
- Your **Moon sign** (emotional and physical body)
- Your **Rising sign** (physical constitution and outer expression)
- The positions of planets like Mars (energy, inflammation) and Saturn (bones, structure)

You don't need to understand everything all at once. Learning astrology is like learning a language; it takes time. Start simply and allow your understanding to grow naturally.

How to Use this Book Along With Your Birth Chart

I have written *Astro Herbalism* as a practical guide—it connects planets to herbs in a way that you can apply directly to your birth chart and to your life.

For example, if you have a strong Mars placement and often experience inflammation, tension, or restlessness, consult the chapter on Mars plants (see pages 54–63) to discover the cooling and grounding herbs that could help. A planet is considered "strong" when it is in its own sign, in an angular house (1st, 4th, 7th, or 10th), or forming multiple aspects with other planets. If you have challenges around Saturn, such as weak bones, low stamina, or feelings of fear and limitation, the chapter on Saturnian plants (see pages 74–83) will introduce you to herbs

♂ ♈

Archetypal Signature *of Mars*

Mars charges us with power, courage, physical stamina, and the capacity for decisive action. Within the astrological chart, it ignites our drive and determination, and governs the way we channel passion, aggression, and ambition.

Mars also dictates how we respond to challenges, conflicts, and obstacles. The planet's position in the birth chart highlights the nature of our physical energy, our approach to pursuing desires, and the tools we use to assert ourselves.

While it grants strength and vitality, excess Mars energy or Mars in difficult aspects to other planets in the birth chart can lead to aggression, impulsiveness, and destructive tendencies. The challenge is understanding how to harness this fiery energy for constructive purposes, ensuring it fuels growth rather than harm.

In Jungian psychology, Mars can reflect parts of the shadow aspects of the psyche, such as unbridled aggression, defensiveness, and the fight-or-flight response. It also represents the warrior archetype within us—the part that defends boundaries, fights for what it values, and pursues personal goals with determination. This archetype, when balanced, supports self-assertion and courage. When imbalanced, it can manifest as anger, recklessness, or burnout.

Mars is considered a malefic planet due to its association with inflammation, accidents, and excessive heat within the body and psyche. It governs the muscular system, motor nerves, and the production of adrenaline, influencing how we catalyze energy, handle stress, and assert ourselves in the world. However, when someone is going through a hard-aspected Mars transit in a chart, or Mars' energy is excessive, it can lead to emotional upheaval, inflammation, high blood pressure, metabolic imbalance, and physical injuries such as fractures or muscle tears.

In mythology, Mars is personified by Ares, the Greek god of war, embodying the raw, unrefined aspects of conflict and power. Ares' narrative often illustrates the destructive potential of unchecked aggression, but also highlights the need

56 Mars: Action and Strength

for courage and action. His fiery and impulsive nature reminds us that while passion and drive are essential for growth, they must be tempered with mindfulness and balance.

When to Use

Work with the energy of Mars when you need to summon courage, physical strength, and decisive action. Mars is particularly supportive during periods of inertia, self-doubt, or lack of direction, providing the energy and determination needed to overcome challenges and pursue goals.

This energy is also invaluable when navigating situations that require assertiveness, setting boundaries, or standing up for oneself. Mars strengthens resilience and promotes endurance, helping you persevere through adversity and emerge stronger. However, caution should be exercised when working with Mars energy during times of heightened stress, anger, or physical depletion, as it may exacerbate feelings of volatility or burnout.

Astrological Correspondences

Birth Chart

Mars Rules: Primarily associated with the Zodiac sign Aries, emphasizing themes of action and courage.

Exalted in Capricorn: Mars expresses disciplined and constructive energy, channeling its drive into long-term goals and achievements.

Detriment in Libra: Mars' assertive nature may struggle in Libra, where harmony and diplomacy are prioritized.

Organs

Muscular System: Governs physical strength and mobility.

Adrenal Glands: Influences adrenaline production, energy bursts, and the stress response.

Blood: Represents vitality, heat, and the circulation of energy.

Systems

Motor Nerves: Regulates action and movement.

Inflammatory Response: Oversees the body's defense mechanisms and reaction to injury or infection.

Hormonal Balance: Particularly linked to testosterone and other sex hormones.

58 Mars: Action and Strength

Plants *of Mars*

Mars' planetary energy serves as a double-edged sword: it can propel us forward with strength and determination or overwhelm us with recklessness and anger. Herbs associated with Mars often share its fiery, invigorating qualities; however, their potent nature requires mindful use to avoid adverse effects. For instance, excess Mars energy can manifest as chronic inflammation, adrenal exhaustion, or emotional volatility. Learning to work with Mars energy involves channeling its intensity into productive and harmonious outlets.

Sweet Basil

(*Ocimum basilicum*)

Medicinal Properties Basil's warming and stimulating qualities align with Mars' energy. It aids digestion, reduces inflammation, and acts as an adaptogen, helping the body respond to stress. Basil is also known for its antimicrobial and immune-boosting properties, making it a powerful ally during periods of physical exertion or recovery.

Celestial Significance Sweet basil carries the energy of a protector and purifier, burning away negative influences and strengthening resilience. Its energy promotes mental clarity, focus, and resilience, helping individuals overcome obstacles and stay committed to their goals.

How to Use Herbal teas, infused oils, cooking, protection rituals, focus-enhancing meditation.

Caution Basil essential oil should be used sparingly and diluted, as excessive amounts can irritate the skin and mucus membranes.

Plants of Mars 59

Archetypal Signature
Archetypal astrology provides insight on your life, which is influenced by celestial movements at the time of your birth.

Astrological Correspondences
Discover the key connections between the planetary archetypes and our bodies.

that can help you to build strength, boundaries, and resilience. Or if your Moon is sensitive or placed in a sign that struggles with nourishment, such as Capricorn, turn to the chapter on lunar herbs that support digestion, hydration, and emotional balance (see pages 24–33).

You will also learn how different planetary herbs can support you during difficult transits, seasonal changes, or times of personal transformation. And a final chapter gives ideas and step-by-step recipes for a range of practical applications, from teas and tinctures to oils and rituals (see pages 112–126).

Think of this book as a guide to building your personal herbal toolkit, one that aligns with your unique astrological signature.

Plants Tap into the medicinal and spiritual properties of the plants closely associated with the celestial bodies in the sky.

Practical applications Integrate astrological herbalism into your daily life with teas, rituals, baths, and more.

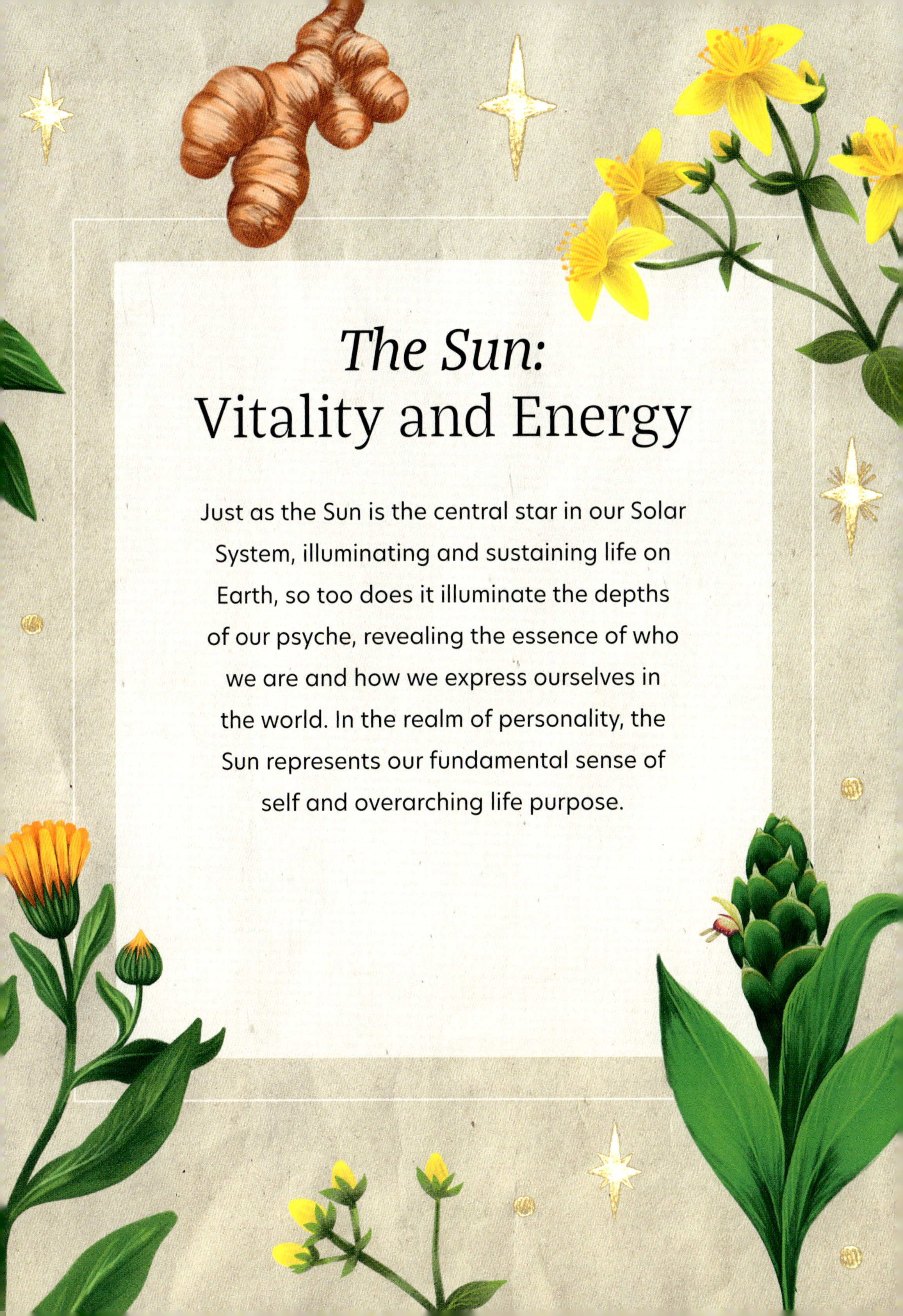

The Sun: Vitality and Energy

Just as the Sun is the central star in our Solar System, illuminating and sustaining life on Earth, so too does it illuminate the depths of our psyche, revealing the essence of who we are and how we express ourselves in the world. In the realm of personality, the Sun represents our fundamental sense of self and overarching life purpose.

Archetypal Signature *of the Sun*

The Sun sign and its position in the birth chart indicate where we draw our strength and confidence. It highlights the most prominent aspects of our personality, reflecting not only who we are but also what we aspire to become. The Sun sign reveals the areas in which we are naturally talented, as well as the qualities we need to develop and refine. It illuminates the core traits that define us and the behaviors to which we are most inclined.

In Jungian psychology, the concept of the ego is closely intertwined with the symbolism of the Sun. The ego represents the conscious aspect of our psyche—the "I" or "self" that navigates the external world and interacts with others. Like the Sun, the ego serves as the focal point of our consciousness, shaping our desires, perceptions, and ambitions. It is through the lens of the ego that we interpret our experiences, form our identity, and assert our individuality in the world.

The ego indicates our innate strengths, talents, and core values, shaping the way we perceive ourselves and interact with others. Individuals with a prominent Sun placement in their birth chart often exude confidence, vitality, and a strong sense of self-assurance. They are driven by a deep-seated desire to express their unique identity and make a significant impact on the world around them.

In Greek mythology, the Sun is personified by the Titan Helios and associated with the god Apollo, the radiant deity of light, music, and prophecy. Apollo is often depicted as a handsome and charismatic figure, adorned with a golden lyre and radiant halo, symbolizing his association with creativity, enlightenment, and divine inspiration. Helios is responsible for driving his chariot across the sky each day, bringing light and warmth to the Earth below. His journey represents the cyclical nature of life and the eternal renewal of vitality and energy.

The correspondence between the Sun and the cardiovascular system is rooted in the symbolism of the heart as the seat of vitality and life-force energy. In ancient Greek medical philosophy, particularly in

the work of Galen, in the 2nd century CE, the heart is revered as the center of our emotional and spiritual well-being, representing the essence of our being and our capacity for love, joy, and also human connection.

As the primary organ responsible for circulating blood throughout the body, the heart is linked to our physical vitality and overall health. Herbs associated with the Sun are revered for their ability to strengthen the heart, uplift the spirit, and enhance vitality.

When to Use

Utilize the energy of the Sun when addressing aspects of self-perception, identity, and ego development. It is especially beneficial for infusing the body with vitality and promoting overall life force. Work with this energy to support your efforts in manifesting goals, dreams, and intentions into reality. The Sun's influence stimulates creative expression, inspiration, and innovation, creating a positive self-image and promoting self-acceptance and self-love. Additionally, it strengthens resilience, empowering you to bounce back from challenges, adversity, and setbacks.

This energy can be particularly helpful in moments of disconnection from your sense of identity or higher self, as well as during periods of lacking purpose. It serves to guide individuals who find themselves operating from a space of performance and people-pleasing, rather than expressing their authentic selves.

Astrological Correspondences

Birth chart

Sun Rules: Primarily associated with the Zodiac sign Leo, emphasizing themes of self-expression, leadership, and vitality.

Exalted in Aries: Amplifies the Sun's qualities of initiative, courage, and assertiveness.

Detriment in Aquarius: Can diminish the Sun's influence, potentially leading to challenges in expressing individuality and creativity.

Organs

Heart: Central to the cardiovascular system, symbolizing vitality, emotional expression, and the seat of love and compassion.

Systems

Metabolism: Influences the body's ability to convert food into energy, supporting vitality and overall health.

Immunity: Plays a vital role in defending the body against pathogens and maintaining optimal health and wellness.

Cardiovascular: Governs the heart and blood vessels, essential for circulating oxygen and nutrients throughout the body.

Plants *of the Sun*

Discover how herbs like St. John's wort, ginger, orange, calendula, and turmeric embody the Sun's radiant energy, offering holistic healing and spiritual nourishment.

St. John's Wort

(Hypericum perforatum)

Medicinal Properties St. John's wort is renowned for its wide array of medicinal properties, making it a versatile herb in natural medicine. It is notably valued for its mood-elevating effects, effectively relieving symptoms of anxiety and depression. Additionally, it exhibits antiviral properties, making it beneficial for fighting off infections, particularly those affecting the respiratory system. It possesses analgesic properties, providing relief from pain and inflammation.

Celestial Significance Historically, St. John's wort has been used as a protective plant against negative energies and psychic disturbances. St. John's wort corresponds to the archetype of the Sun due to its vibrant yellow flowers and its association with light and vitality. Like the Sun, it exudes warmth, optimism, and energy, symbolizing the essence of vitality and life force. It is believed to ward off darkness and negativity, inviting blessings and abundance into one's life. Working with St. John's wort can cultivate a sense of inner light and resilience.

How to Use Herbal infusions or teas, tinctures, capsules, dreamwork, and visioning.

Caution St. John's wort can interact with certain medications, including antidepressants and birth control.

Calendula

(Calendula officinalis)

Medicinal Properties Calendula, also known as pot marigold, is esteemed for its remarkable medicinal properties, rendering it a staple in natural remedies. Its primary use lies in its potent anti-inflammatory and antiseptic properties, which make it invaluable for promoting wound healing and 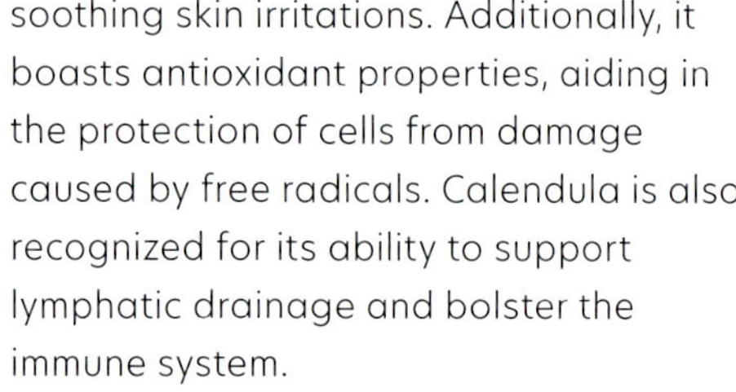 soothing skin irritations. Additionally, it boasts antioxidant properties, aiding in the protection of cells from damage caused by free radicals. Calendula is also recognized for its ability to support lymphatic drainage and bolster the immune system.

Celestial Significance Calendula is believed to ward off negative energies and promote spiritual well-being, inviting blessings and prosperity into one's life. Historically, it has been utilized for its protective qualities, guarding against malevolent energies and promoting overall wellness.

How to Use Teas, infused oils, incense, tinctures, charms, and protection rituals.

> Historically, calendula has been utilized for its protective qualities, guarding against malevolent energies.

Turmeric

(Curcuma longa)

Medicinal Properties Turmeric, famous for its vibrant golden hue and potent medicinal properties, is renowned as a powerhouse herb in natural medicine. Its primary active compound, curcumin, boasts powerful anti-inflammatory and antioxidant properties, making it effective in reducing inflammation, combating oxidative stress, and supporting overall immune function. Turmeric is widely used to alleviate symptoms of arthritis, improve digestion, and promote cardiovascular health. Additionally, it exhibits antimicrobial properties, aiding in the prevention and treatment of infections.

Celestial Significance Spiritually, turmeric is revered as a symbol of abundance, prosperity, and spiritual awakening. Its golden color symbolizes the radiant energy of the Sun, infusing the spirit with warmth, optimism, and divine light. Turmeric is believed to purify the body, mind, and spirit, cleansing away any negativity and opening the heart to love and abundance.

How to Use Golden milk, turmeric tea, mindful cooking, and solar plexus meditation.

Turmeric is believed to purify the body, mind, and spirit.

Ginger

(Zingiber officinale)

Medicinal Properties Ginger is a highly valued medicinal herb known for its wide-ranging benefits, particularly in supporting the digestive system and combating inflammation. It is commonly used to alleviate nausea, improve digestion, and reduce bloating. Its potent anti-inflammatory properties make it effective in relieving pain associated with arthritis and muscle soreness. Ginger also acts as a natural stimulant, invigorating the circulatory system and helping to ward off colds and respiratory infections. Additionally, it enhances immune function and has antioxidant properties that protect the body from cellular damage.

Celestial Significance Due to its warming and stimulating nature, ginger aligns with the solar qualities of energy, vitality, and personal power. It embodies radiant heat, invigorating the body and spirit, and is often used to invoke willpower, courage, and confidence. Spiritually, ginger is regarded as a catalyst for transformation, helping individuals overcome inertia and step into their full potential. Its fiery nature stimulates passion, personal growth, and motivation, driving forward action and manifestation.

How to Use Teas, infused oils, tinctures, mindful cooking, as a circulatory stimulant, and in warming rituals.

Orange

(Citrus × sinensis)

Medicinal Properties Oranges, which are rich in vitamin C, are a powerful ally in boosting the immune system and protecting against colds and infections. Their high antioxidant content helps neutralize free radicals, reducing inflammation and promoting overall cellular health. Oranges are also known to support heart health by lowering cholesterol and improving circulation. Additionally, the essential oils in orange peel offer anti-inflammatory and antibacterial properties, making them useful in skin care for reducing acne and promoting skin healing. The refreshing and zesty nature of oranges lifts the mood and energizes the body, making them a popular remedy for mental exhaustion and fatigue.

Celestial Significance Oranges are associated with happiness, abundance, and creativity, symbolizing the Sun's ability to inspire growth and prosperity. In spiritual practices, oranges are often used to attract positivity, joy, and wealth, amplifying the flow of creative energy and enhancing personal magnetism. The scent and presence of oranges can clear negative energy, uplifting the spirit and promoting a sense of joy and renewal.

How to Use Fresh juice, essential oils for aromatherapy, incense, offerings, and prosperity rituals.

> Oranges are often used to attract positivity, joy, and wealth.

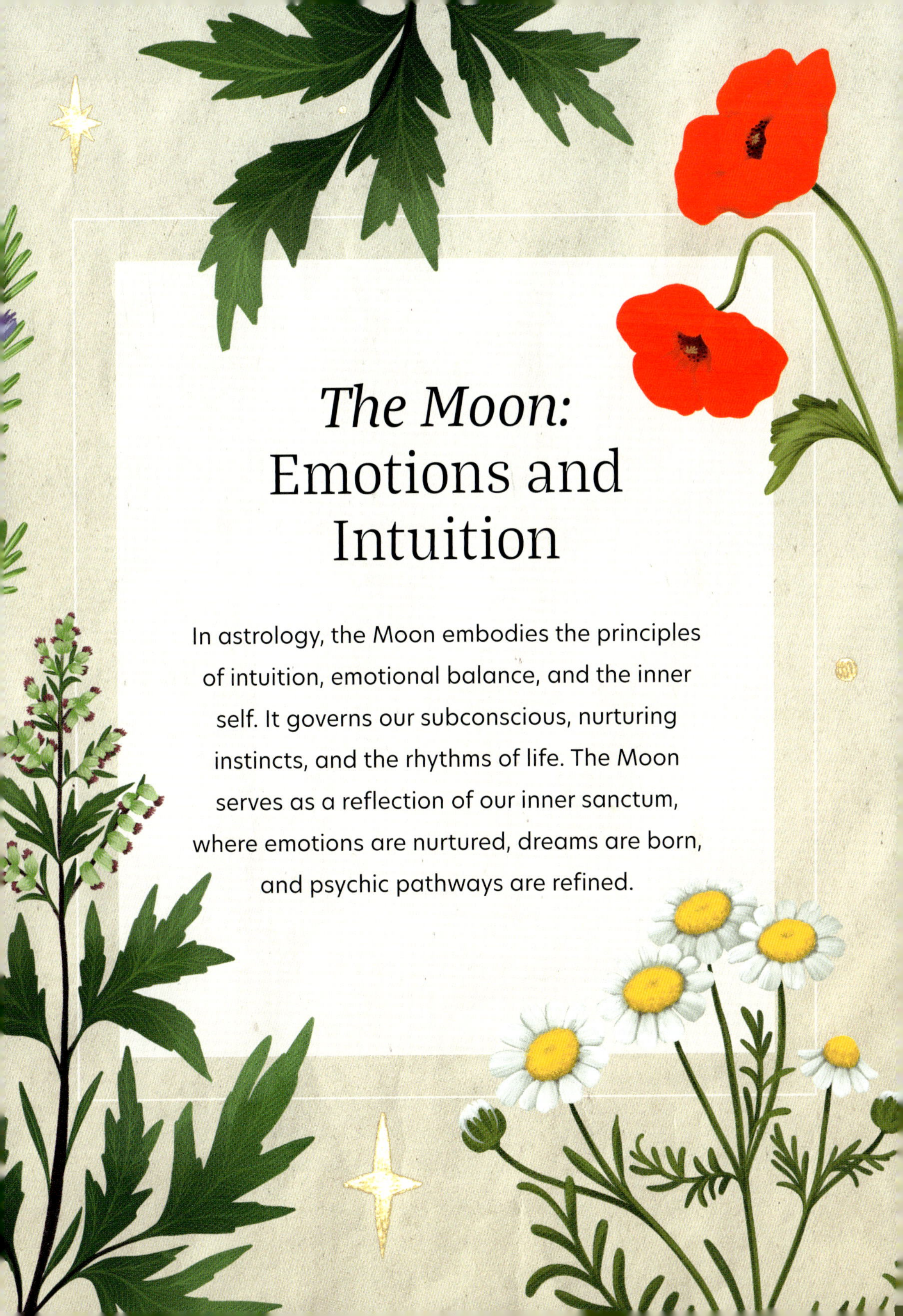

The Moon: Emotions and Intuition

In astrology, the Moon embodies the principles of intuition, emotional balance, and the inner self. It governs our subconscious, nurturing instincts, and the rhythms of life. The Moon serves as a reflection of our inner sanctum, where emotions are nurtured, dreams are born, and psychic pathways are refined.

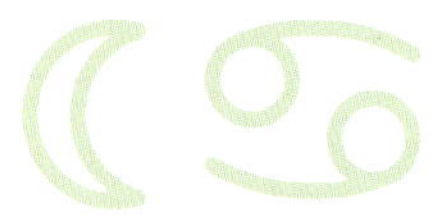

Archetypal Signature *of the Moon*

The Moon's position in a natal chart offers insight into our most vulnerable and emotionally charged areas. It reveals how we care for ourselves and others, guiding us to understand our deepest needs for comfort, security, and connection. The Moon teaches us to honor cycles of rest, reflection, and renewal, paralleling its waxing and waning phases in the night sky.

The Moon connects to the unconscious—the reservoir of thoughts, memories, and experiences that exist beneath the surface of our awareness. The unconscious shapes much of our emotional life, influencing how we react to the world and how we process experiences. Emotions often arise from the unconscious, carrying the imprints of past events, ancestral patterns, and primal instincts. These emotions may surface unexpectedly, guiding us to explore and integrate hidden parts of ourselves.

From a Jungian perspective, the Moon aligns with the "anima," or the inner feminine aspect of the psyche, which encompasses the intuitive, emotional, and nurturing parts of our being. Its symbolism is about exploring the hidden layers of the subconscious, aiming for emotional balance and psychic awareness.

The Moon also governs intuition—the inner knowing that transcends logic and connects us to a deeper sense of truth. Intuition is often described as a "gut feeling," a subtle yet powerful sense of understanding or awareness that guides our choices and perceptions. It emerges when we quiet the noise of the conscious mind and attune to the wisdom of the subconscious. Strengthening intuition involves cultivating stillness, practicing mindfulness, and trusting the subtle cues and signals from within. Activities such as meditation, journaling, dreamwork, and working with lunar herbs can deepen our intuitive abilities, allowing us to access the guidance of our inner voice.

The Moon teaches us about cycles—both celestial and personal. Its phases mirror the rhythm of life: waxing, waning, and returning to fullness, symbolizing growth, release, and renewal.

The Moon's cycles resonate deeply with the menstrual cycle, a connection to nature's rhythms.

In mythology, lunar deities such as Artemis, Selene, and Hecate represent the Moon's themes of protection, introspection, and transformation. These goddesses guard the thresholds of the unseen, offering wisdom and guidance in the realms of intuition, dreams, and the mysteries of the psyche.

When to Use

Use the energy of the Moon when you are seeking emotional balance, want to strengthen your intuition, or feel the need to connect with your inner self. It is especially helpful for reflecting on your feelings, understanding your emotions, and exploring your dreams.

Work with lunar energy to enhance your awareness, develop your psychic abilities, and move through life's changes with ease. The Moon's energy can support you when you are feeling emotionally vulnerable, helping you to process and release feelings buried in your subconscious. It is also helpful when you need comfort, peace, or clarity in times of emotional stress or confusion.

This energy is particularly useful when you feel disconnected from your inner self or intuition, or when life feels out of balance. The Moon encourages you to align with natural rhythms and cycles, restoring harmony to your life. For women, the Moon's energy can help you connect with your menstrual cycle, empowering you to embrace your natural rhythms and inner wisdom.

Astrological Correspondences

Birth chart

Moon Rules: Associated with Cancer, reflecting emotional depth, intuition, and nurturing instincts.

Exalted in Taurus: Amplifies the Moon's grounding and stabilizing qualities, fostering emotional security.

Detriment in Capricorn: Challenges emotional expression and vulnerability, emphasizing responsibility over sentiment.

Organs

Stomach and Digestive System: Governs nourishment and digestion, reflecting the emotional connection to food and care.

Lungs: Symbolizes the rhythmic nature of breath, aligning with emotional regulation and release.

Systems

Reproductive: Reflects the Moon's association with cycles of fertility, creation, and hormonal balance.

Nervous: Supports emotional resilience and balance, soothing stress and promoting inner calm.

Plants *of the Moon*

Herbs associated with the Moon resonate with its nurturing and reflective qualities. These plants support emotional balance, enhance intuition, and connect us to the dream world, helping us to navigate the inner landscapes of our spirit with grace and clarity. Plants that are allied with lunar energy–such as chamomile, mugwort, poppy, rosemary, and white rose–support emotional balance, reflection, and a deeper connection to your inner self.

Chamomile

(Matricaria recutita)

Medicinal Properties Chamomile, also known as scented mayweed, is widely known for its calming effects on the nervous system, helping to ease anxiety, stress, and restlessness. It is a gentle herb often used to promote restful sleep and relaxation, making it a great ally during times of emotional upheaval. Chamomile also has anti-inflammatory and digestive properties, helping to soothe stomach issues and support overall gut health, which is linked to emotional well-being.

Celestial Significance Chamomile embodies the nurturing, soothing qualities of the Moon. Its gentle energy helps calm turbulent emotions and encourages emotional healing. Chamomile's ability to promote relaxation and harmony mirrors the Moon's role in balancing our inner worlds, guiding us toward self-care and emotional clarity.

How to Use Calming bedtime tea, relaxing bath soak, facial steam, and in dream pillows.

Mugwort

(Artemisia vulgaris)

Medicinal Properties Mugwort, also known as common wormwood, is a versatile herb often used for anxiety, insomnia, pain relief, digestion, and the regulation of menstrual cycles. It also supports liver health and energy levels. In Traditional Chinese Medicine, it is used to enhance the effects of acupuncture.

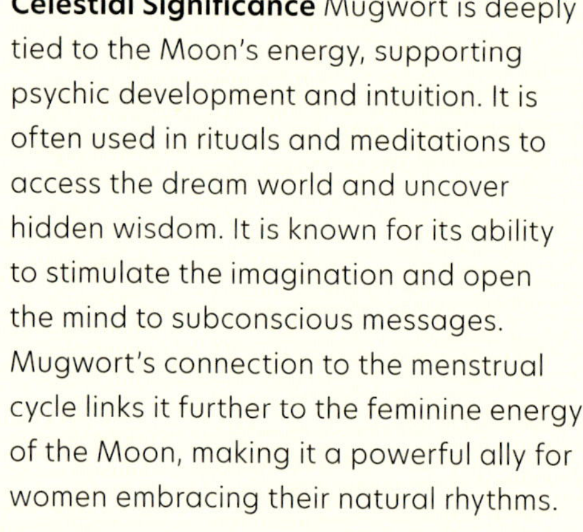

Celestial Significance Mugwort is deeply tied to the Moon's energy, supporting psychic development and intuition. It is often used in rituals and meditations to access the dream world and uncover hidden wisdom. It is known for its ability to stimulate the imagination and open the mind to subconscious messages. Mugwort's connection to the menstrual cycle links it further to the feminine energy of the Moon, making it a powerful ally for women embracing their natural rhythms.

How to Use Cleansing smudge, teas or tinctures, moon rituals; add to dream pillows or place under the pillow.

Caution Be mindful that mugwort may cause an allergic reaction in people with ragweed allergies as well as allergies to celery, carrot, or birch. Do not use if you have allergies to any of these plants.

Poppy

(Papaver somniferum)

Medicinal Properties Poppy is known for its calming and sedative effects, helping to ease insomnia, stress, and nervous tension. Its gentle, dreamlike energy allows for emotional release and introspection. Poppy seeds are also rich in nutrients that support overall health, while the plant itself has historically been associated with inducing states of rest and relaxation.

Celestial Significance Poppy carries the Moon's dreamy, mystical energy, offering a sense of peace and calm. It symbolizes the dream state and the boundary between the conscious and subconscious. Poppy encourages the letting go of worries and trusting in the natural cycles of rest and renewal.

> Poppy encourages the letting go of worries and trusting in the natural cycles of rest and renewal.

How to Use Add seeds to pastries, breads and desserts; meditative rituals; lunar celebration offerings, and calming bath blends.

Caution Infusing the seeds in water or oils for ingestion is not recommended, as the potency and effects can vary greatly depending on the source and preparation.

Rosemary

(Salvia rosmarinus)

Medicinal Properties Rosemary is a stimulating herb known to improve memory, focus, and mental clarity. It also supports circulation and digestion, while providing a gentle boost to the immune system. Its aromatic properties uplift the spirit and create a sense of mental and emotional balance.

Celestial Significance Rosemary's connection to memory, wisdom, and emotional grounding aligns it with the Moon's reflective qualities. Rosemary helps to bridge the conscious and subconscious, supporting emotional integration and allowing us to access the inner knowledge stored in the body and psyche.

In lunar terms, rosemary can be seen as a herb that protects and preserves the inner landscape. It offers psychic containment, helping to hold memory and emotion without becoming overwhelmed.

This reflects the Moon's role in psychic digestion, the way we absorb, process, and respond to past experiences. It is particularly supportive during personal phases of grief, reflection, or emotional contraction. In these moments, rosemary acts as a stabilizer of internal tides.

How to Use Burn as an incense, use in teas or tinctures, add to bathwater, and in moon rituals.

White Rose

(Rosa × alba)

Medicinal Properties White roses, such as the white rose of York, are revered for their soothing and uplifting properties; they are used to calm the heart, relieve stress, and encourage emotional healing. Their anti-inflammatory and antioxidant qualities also make them valuable for skin care, while their scent promotes relaxation and inner peace.

Celestial Significance White roses embody the Moon's purity and softness, symbolizing peace, intuition, and emotional balance. They are a reminder of the beauty in vulnerability and the importance of nurturing one's emotional self. White roses connect us to the spiritual aspects of the Moon, enhancing clarity and bringing calm.

How to Use Teas, bath rituals, altar offering, and meditative practices.

White roses connect us to the spiritual aspects of the Moon, enhancing clarity and bringing calm.

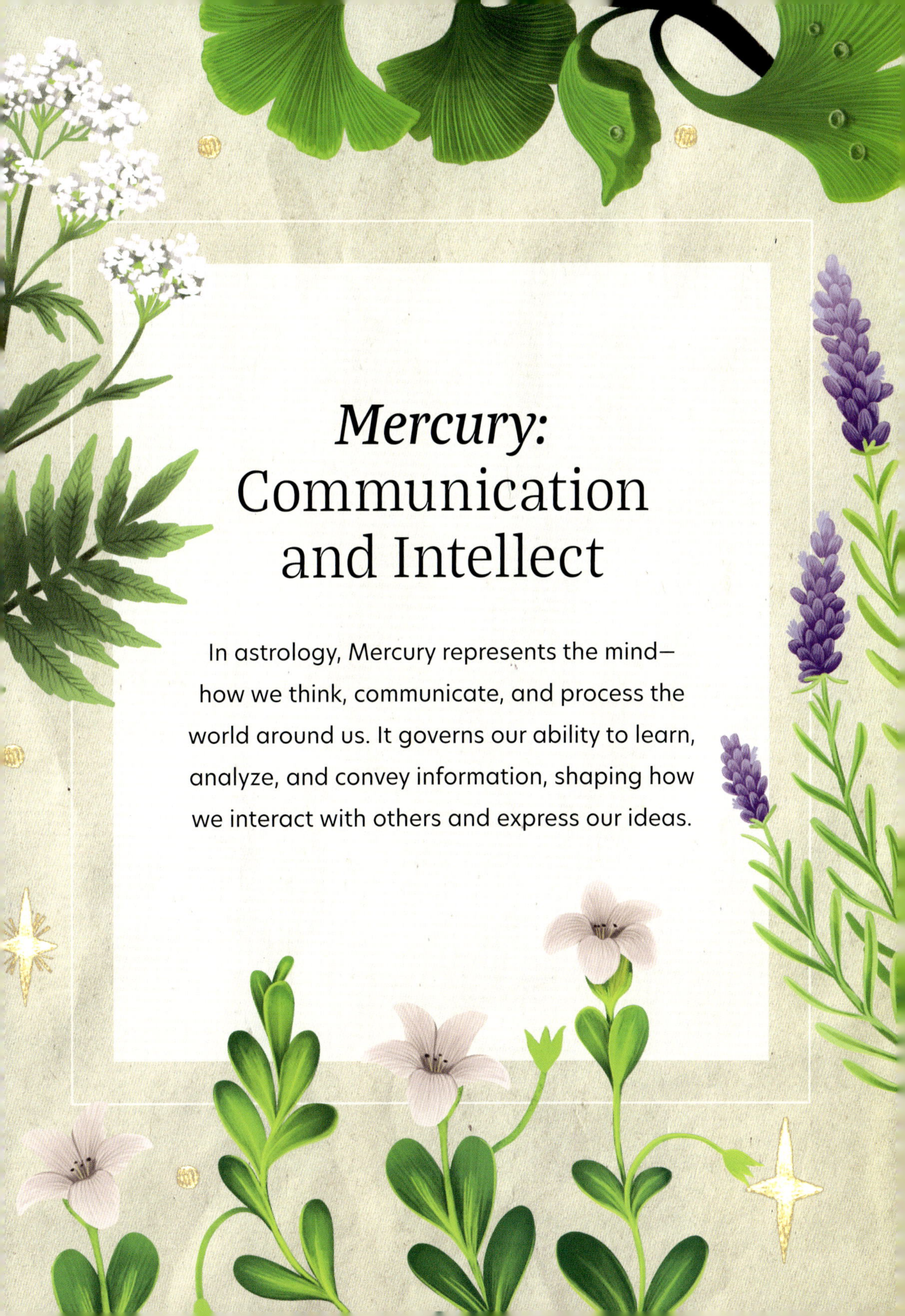

Mercury: Communication and Intellect

In astrology, Mercury represents the mind—how we think, communicate, and process the world around us. It governs our ability to learn, analyze, and convey information, shaping how we interact with others and express our ideas.

☿ ♊ ♍

Archetypal Signature *of Mercury*

Mercury's position in a natal chart shows how we process and interpret life. It speaks to how we absorb and analyze information, the ways in which we express our thoughts, and the tools we use to understand and connect with the world. Just as Mercury, the Roman deity, moved between realms to deliver messages, so the energy of his planetary namesake connects the inner workings of our minds to the outer world through speech, writing, and other forms of communication.

This connection is not just practical but also deeply symbolic: Mercury represents the bridge between our unconscious mind and conscious expression. It carries messages from our shadow self—the undiscovered parts of who we are—into the world of our manifested self, shaping our voice and how we share our inner truth.

In addition to communication, Mercury's energy enhances curiosity and adaptability. It encourages quick thinking, problem-solving, and the ability to see different perspectives, making it a planet of the mind.

When to Use

The energy of Mercury is especially useful when clarity of thought is needed. It can help in moments when mental focus feels difficult to maintain, or when you need to organize ideas and express them clearly. Working with Mercury can be helpful during times when communication feels strained, offering support for speaking openly, listening carefully, and resolving misunderstandings.

Mercury's influence can also be beneficial when the mind is feeling overstimulated or stuck in overthinking. It encourages a sense of calm, helping you to slow down and reflect, while still staying engaged and productive. When faced with decisions, Mercury helps to untangle conflicting thoughts and supports clear, logical choices.

For those seeking inspiration, Mercury's energy sparks curiosity and creativity. It helps uncover new perspectives and allows for better problem-solving, especially when adapting to unexpected changes or challenges. Mercury's connection

to the nervous system also makes it a powerful guide during times of stress, helping to ease mental strain and restore a sense of ease.

Mercury's influence is particularly potent during transitions, negotiations, and learning processes. Whether you're starting a new project, studying a subject in depth, or trying to navigate conflicts or upsetting conversations, Mercury's archetype can help you move through the unknown with more awareness and adaptability.

In Jungian terms, Mercury reflects the archetype of the trickster and the psychopomp—the one who guides us through the liminal spaces between what is known and unknown. This makes Mercury especially powerful during periods of inner questioning, therapy, or self-inquiry, when unconscious material begins to rise to the surface.

Energetically, Mercury governs the body's way of registering and responding to the environment. When these systems feel dysregulated, Mercury-aligned practices or herbs can support our capacity to stay mentally aware without becoming overwhelmed.

Astrological Correspondences

Birth chart

Mercury Rules: Associated with Gemini and Virgo, highlighting themes of quick thinking, analysis, and communication.

Exalted in Virgo: Enhances Mercury's precision, organization, and attention to detail.

Detriment in Aries and Scorpio: May bring challenges with focus, leading to scattered thoughts or difficulty in clear communication.

Organs

Nervous System: Reflects Mercury's role in transmitting and processing information.

Lungs: Tied to breath and voice, which are essential for communication and expression.

Systems

Cognitive: Supports focus, memory, and learning.

Digestive: Connects to Virgo, symbolizing the assimilation of information, as well as physical nutrients.

Plants *of* Mercury

The energy of Mercury helps us make sense of the information that we gather through our five senses, allowing us to turn observations into thoughts and ideas. As such, herbs associated with the planet–including brahmi, cardamom, ginkgo, lavender, and valerian–promote mental clarity, clear expression, and calmness during times of mental stress.

Brahmi

(Bacopa monnieri)

Medicinal Properties Also known as the "herb of grace," this powerful plant is well-known for improving brain health, focus, and memory. Brahmi supports cognitive function, reduces mental fatigue, and helps to manage stress. It is also known for calming the nervous system, allowing the mind to stay clear and alert without feeling overstimulated.

Celestial Significance Brahmi embodies Mercury's qualities of intellect, clarity, and adaptability. It encourages the free flow of thought and supports a balanced, alert mind. Traditionally used in practices like Ayurveda to enhance concentration and meditation, brahmi aligns with Mercury's ability to bridge the gap between the internal world of ideas and external communication.

How to Use Teas or tinctures, oils for scalp massage, meditative sessions, as a study aid or aid for concentration.

Caution Be aware that brahmi may interact with medications for thyroid disorders, as well as sedatives or anti-anxiety medications, potentially enhancing their effects. Speak to your medical practitioner if using any of these medications.

Cardamom

(Elettaria cardamomum)

Medicinal Properties Cardamom is known for its warming properties, supporting digestion and respiratory health. Its uplifting scent and flavor help to clear mental fog, reduce stress, and bring focus to the mind. It also helps to energize the senses while calming emotional tension.

Celestial Significance Cardamom reflects Mercury's dynamic and versatile energy. Its ability to clear stagnation, both physically and mentally, mirrors Mercury's role in enhancing communication and adaptability. The bright and invigorating qualities of cardamom make it an ideal herb for promoting clarity and focus, helping to align the mind with action.

How to Use Add to teas, coffee, or food; use in a diffuser or as an inhalation blend.

Cardamom's uplifting scent and flavor help to clear mental fog, reduce stress, and bring focus to the mind.

Ginkgo

(Ginkgo biloba)

Medicinal Properties Ginkgo, also known as the maidenhair tree, is widely known for improving blood circulation to the brain, enhancing memory, and supporting cognitive function. The plant is rich in antioxidants, which help to protect the brain from oxidative stress. Ginkgo is often used to maintain mental sharpness and reduce the effects of aging on memory and focus.

Celestial Significance Ginkgo aligns with Mercury's intellectual and quick-moving energy, symbolizing the flow of ideas and sharpness of thought. Its ability to enhance focus and support mental stamina makes it a natural representation of Mercury's influence on the mind. Ginkgo's fan-shaped leaves, resembling the brain's hemispheres, further connect it to themes of intellect and clarity.

Ginkgo is also one of the oldest living tree species on Earth, which speaks to its connection with deep memory and ancestral intelligence. In this way, it doesn't just support short-term cognition, but also helps access stored wisdom across time. This corresponds with Mercury's role not only as the messenger but also as the interpreter of long-held knowledge, translating the past into meaningful insight in the present.

How to Use Teas, in capsule form, in rituals focused on enhancing intellectual abilities.

Caution Ginkgo should be avoided by those taking anticoagulant medications or with bleeding disorders.

Lavender

(*Lavandula* species)

Medicinal Properties With powerful calming effects on the nervous system, lavender helps to relieve stress, anxiety, and mental fatigue. This fragrant herb supports restful sleep, while also maintaining enough clarity to keep the mind engaged and balanced. Lavender is often used for emotional well-being, providing comfort and calmness.

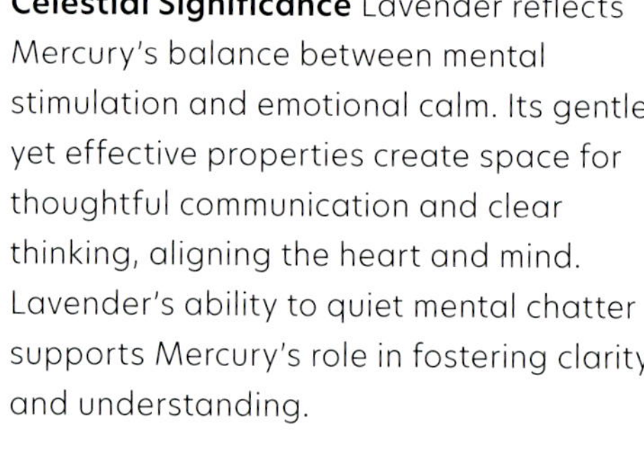

Celestial Significance Lavender reflects Mercury's balance between mental stimulation and emotional calm. Its gentle yet effective properties create space for thoughtful communication and clear thinking, aligning the heart and mind. Lavender's ability to quiet mental chatter supports Mercury's role in fostering clarity and understanding.

How to Use Teas, in baths, for relaxation rituals and self-reflection meditation; the essential oil can be diffused or applied topically.

> Lavender helps to relieve stress, anxiety, and mental fatigue.

Valerian

(Valeriana officinalis)

Medicinal Properties Common or garden valerian is a powerful herb for calming the nervous system, helping to ease stress and improve quality of sleep. It is particularly useful for quieting overactive thoughts and reducing feelings of anxiety. Its sedative effects make it a go-to remedy for restoring mental and emotional balance.

Celestial Significance Valerian mirrors Mercury's capacity to mediate and balance opposing forces. By soothing an overactive mind and grounding restless energy, it allows for greater focus and clarity. Valerian's ability to calm without dulling the mind supports Mercury's qualities of sharpness and adaptability.

How to Use Teas or tinctures.

Caution Avoid combining valerian with alcohol, sedatives, or other medications that depress the nervous system. Avoid any activity that require alertness, such as driving or operating heavy machinery, after consumption.

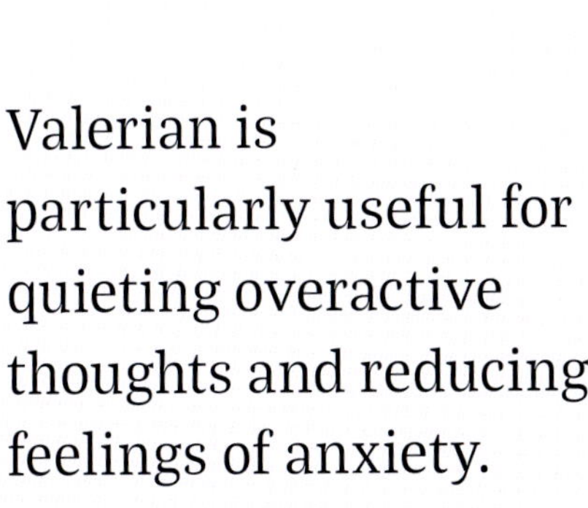

> Valerian is particularly useful for quieting overactive thoughts and reducing feelings of anxiety.

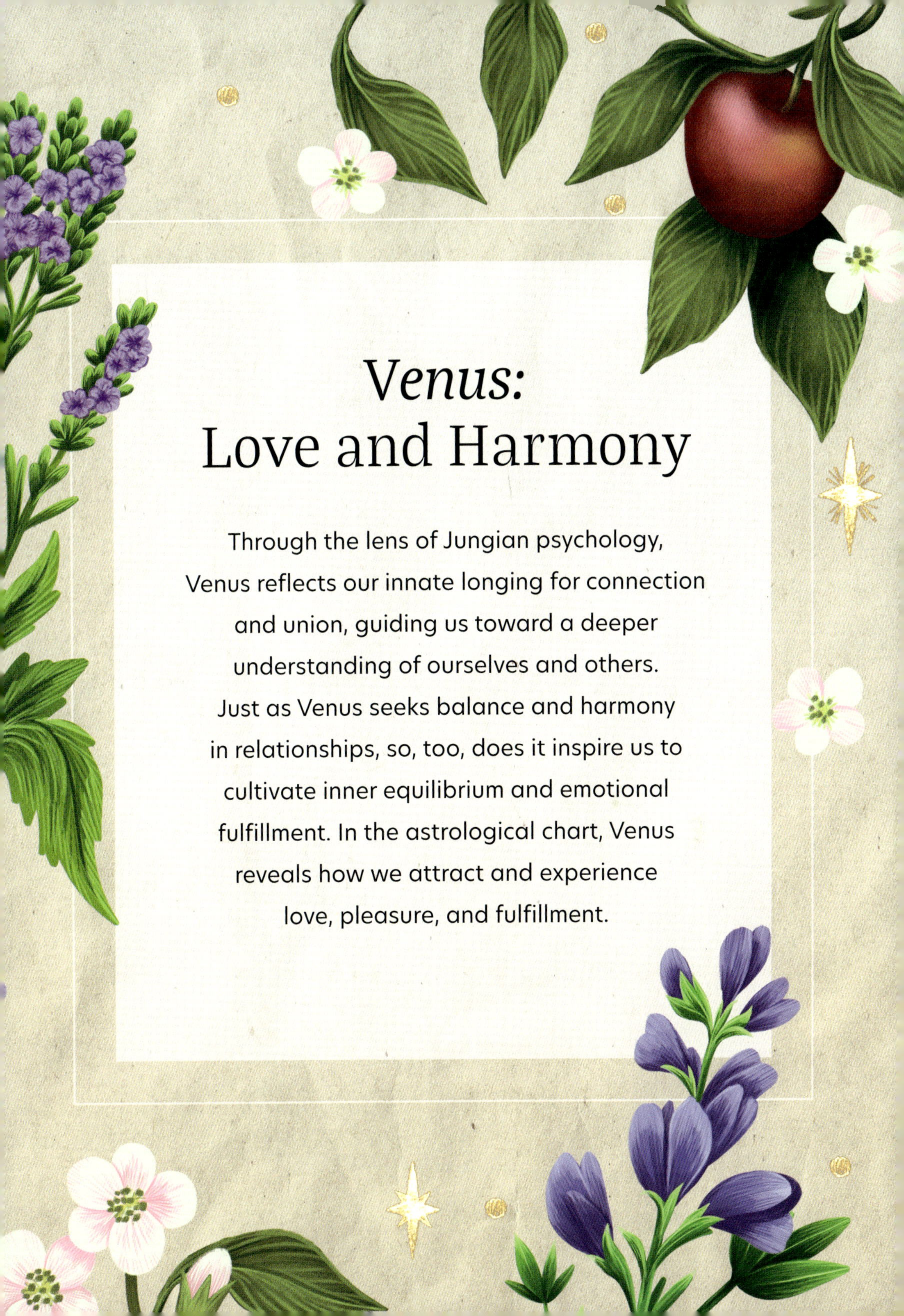

Venus: Love and Harmony

Through the lens of Jungian psychology, Venus reflects our innate longing for connection and union, guiding us toward a deeper understanding of ourselves and others. Just as Venus seeks balance and harmony in relationships, so, too, does it inspire us to cultivate inner equilibrium and emotional fulfillment. In the astrological chart, Venus reveals how we attract and experience love, pleasure, and fulfillment.

♀ ♉ ♎

Archetypal Signature *of Venus*

The placement and aspects of Venus in our astrological chart sheds light on our romantic inclinations, aesthetic preferences, and values in relationships. Individuals with strong Venus placements may prioritize harmony, beauty, and sensual pleasures. Conversely, challenging aspects to Venus may indicate struggles with self-worth, codependency, or unrealistic expectations in relationships.

In Greek mythology, Venus is personified as Aphrodite, the goddess of love, beauty, and fertility. According to legend, Aphrodite emerged from the sea foam, radiating beauty and allure wherever she went. Her divine presence inspired passion and desire, captivating gods and mortals alike. Aphrodite's myth embodies the transformative power of love and the universal longing for connection and intimacy.

In regard to the planet, Venus is also associated with the concept of beauty, yet its influence goes far beyond mere appearances. Venus governs what captures our attention and evokes our sense of aesthetic pleasure. What each of us finds beautiful varies widely, and this subjective attraction reflects a profound psychological process.

When viewed in the context of Jungian psychology, Venus becomes a symbol of the projection mechanism—what we find beautiful in the external world mirrors hidden or undiscovered aspects of our inner psyche. These external attractions serve as keys to uncovering deeper layers of ourselves, revealing both the conscious and unconscious qualities we appreciate.

Venus invites us to explore what we value, desire, and seek to attract in our lives, offering insight into our individual paths of self-discovery. What we consider beautiful or pleasurable—whether a person, a song, a piece of art, or even a shared experience—carries within it a resonance with our inner world. These connections are not arbitrary, but rather mirrors that reflect parts of ourselves we are either fully aware of or have yet to recognize. Jungian psychology suggests that through such projections, we engage in a process of individuation, as these external reflections guide us toward a

deeper understanding of who we are and who we have the potential to become.

Venusian herbs play a pivotal role in promoting beauty, pleasure, and emotional well-being. These herbs not only support our aesthetic pursuits but also nourish the spirit, providing feelings of bliss, happiness, and euphoria. Additionally, Venusian herbs are associated with the kidneys, which play a vital role in maintaining fluid balance and emotional equilibrium in the body.

When to Use

Harness the power of Venus when working with the principle of balance, fostering symbiosis between elements and promoting equilibrium and harmony. Venus is also helpful when navigating the relational realm, fostering connections with others as well as with ourselves.

Venusian plants possess the unique ability to heal our emotional and spiritual hearts, assisting us in clarifying and identifying wounds and patterns formed through past relationship dynamics. These plants help us connect with the vibration of love and joy, elevating our energetic frequencies and facilitating the attraction of individuals who resonate more harmoniously with us.

Astrological Correspondences

Birth chart

Venus Rules: Primarily associated with Taurus and Libra, reflecting a connection to sensual pleasures and material comfort in Taurus, while Libra highlights the importance of partnership and social harmony.

Exalted in Pisces: When exalted in Pisces, Venus amplifies qualities of compassion, empathy, and artistic inspiration.

Detriment in Aries and Scorpio: In Scorpio, the intense emotional dynamics can lead to challenges in relationships; while in Aries, the focus may shift to impulsiveness and self-interest.

Organs

Kidneys: Maintains fluid balance and emotional equilibrium within the body. The health of the kidneys is linked to the capacity for love, balance, nurturing, and emotional well-being.

Systems

Reproductive: Venus significantly influences the reproductive system, intimacy, and healthy relationships.

Circulatory: It governs aspects of the circulatory system, symbolizing the flow of love throughout the body.

Plants *of Venus*

Discover how rose, damiana, apple, vervain, and wild indigo support connections and balance the body through the lens of Venus. Venus represents our deepest desires for beauty, pleasure, and meaningful relationships.

Rose

(*Rosa spp.*)

Medicinal Properties Rose is revered for its ability to support emotional healing, promote radiant skin, and calm the nervous system. Rose also has anti-inflammatory and antioxidant properties, making it beneficial for the skin and overall well-being. Additionally, rose can reduce stress, soothe the nervous system, and bring emotional balance, offering comfort during times of grief or heartache.

Celestial Significance In connection with Venus, the rose embodies the principles of love, beauty, and harmony. Its delicate petals and intoxicating scent symbolize tenderness, sensuality, and emotional warmth. Spiritually, rose is a powerful ally for opening the heart to give and receive love, cultivating inner beauty, and nurturing a sense of emotional balance. It's often used to open the heart chakra, encouraging feelings of love, compassion, and self-acceptance. Its energy is gentle yet transformative, helping to dissolve emotional blockages and foster deeper connections with oneself and others.

How to Use Herbal teas, infused oils, skincare, aromatherapy, bath rituals, heart-centered meditations, offerings, and incenses.

Damiana

(Turnera diffusa)

Medicinal Properties Damiana is known for its aphrodisiac qualities and ability to enhance libido and sexual vitality. It can, stimulate desire, support the reproductive system and promote hormonal balance. Damiana also has a calming effect on the nervous system, helping to reduce anxiety, improve mood, and enhance overall well-being. Additionally, it can aid digestion and boost energy levels, making it a versatile herb for both physical and emotional health.

Celestial Significance As a Venusian herb, damiana embodies passion, desire, and sensuality. Its stimulating energy enhances emotional and physical connections, helping individuals embrace their sensuality and deepen intimacy. On a spiritual level, damiana promotes emotional healing and self-acceptance, while encouraging openness to pleasure and love. It is ideal for balancing the energy of relationships, enhancing both self-love and romantic attraction.

How to Use Herbal teas or infusions, tinctures, bath rituals, aphrodisiac elixirs, love rituals, meditations, and offerings.

Apple

(Malus domestica)

Medicinal Properties Apples are highly regarded for their nutritional benefits, offering a wealth of vitamins, minerals, and dietary fiber that support overall health. They are known for their antioxidant properties, which help reduce inflammation, support heart health, and promote healthy digestion. Rich in vitamin C, apples also contribute to immune function and skin health, while their soluble fiber aids in regulating blood sugar levels and improving gut health.

Celestial Significance Apples are often linked to themes of temptation and knowledge, particularly in the biblical story of Eve in the Garden of Eden. However, apples can also be viewed through the lens of Aphrodite, who is associated with the mischievous side of the feminine. The apple embodies both the sweetness of love and the complexity of human relationships, symbolizing the rewards and challenges of intimacy. Thus, apples represent the balance between pleasure and consequence, aligning them closely with Venusian energies.

How to Use Fresh fruit, apple cider, apple juice, infused water, offerings, charms, and sachets.

> The apple embodies both the sweetness of love and the complexity of human relationships.

Vervain

(Verbena officinalis)

Medicinal Properties Vervain, also known as herb of the cross, is revered for its calming and restorative properties, making it a valuable plant in herbal medicine. Known for its ability to reduce stress and anxiety, vervain promotes emotional balance and relaxation. It is often used to support the nervous system, alleviate insomnia, and enhance overall well-being. Additionally, vervain is believed to have anti-inflammatory and analgesic properties, aiding in pain relief and promoting healing.

Celestial Significance In astrology, vervain symbolizes the pursuit of harmony in relationships. It promotes mutual understanding, encourages individuals to embrace vulnerability in their relationships, and enhances emotional connections.

In mythology, vervain is associated with love, protection, and purification. It was historically regarded as a sacred herb, used in rituals to attract love and dispel negativity, protect against evil spells, and clear stagnant energy in relationships and spaces.

How to Use Teas, meditations, bath rituals, protective smudge, incense, charms, and infused oils.

Wild Indigo

(Baptisia tinctoria)

Medicinal Properties Wild indigo, also known as horsefly weed, has powerful immune-boosting properties and supports the body in fighting off infections. Traditionally used in herbal medicine, it is known for its anti-inflammatory and antimicrobial effects, making it beneficial for addressing respiratory issues and promoting overall wellness. Wild indigo is also used as a lymphatic stimulant, helping to cleanse the lymphatic system and enhance the body's natural defenses. It promotes resilience and strength, a reflection of what is needed in the cycles of death and rebirth in both love and relationships.

Celestial Significance Astrologically, wild indigo resonates with themes of protection, courage, and emotional healing. It symbolizes the importance of safeguarding one's emotional boundaries while fostering harmonious relationships. Wild indigo encourages individuals to embrace their strength and assertiveness, which can be essential for navigating the complexities of love and connection.

How to Use Infused oils, tinctures, herbal infusions, cleansing rituals, and charms.

> Wild indigo encourages individuals to embrace their strength and assertiveness.

Mars: Action and Strength

The red planet symbolizes primal energy—the fuel that brings ideas, dreams, and desires into manifestation. Discover how herbs such as sweet basil, black pepper, cat's claw, cinnamon, and nettle embody Mars' fiery essence, offering strength, action, and resilience.

Archetypal Signature *of Mars*

Mars charges us with power, courage, physical stamina, and the capacity for decisive action. Within the astrological chart, it ignites our drive and determination, and governs the way we channel passion, aggression, and ambition.

Mars also dictates how we respond to challenges, conflicts, and obstacles. The planet's position in the birth chart highlights the nature of our physical energy, our approach to pursuing desires, and the tools we use to assert ourselves.

While it grants strength and vitality, excess Mars energy or Mars in difficult aspects to other planets in the birth chart can lead to aggression, impulsiveness, and destructive tendencies. The challenge is understanding how to harness this fiery energy for constructive purposes, ensuring it fuels growth rather than harm.

In Jungian psychology, Mars can reflect parts of the shadow aspects of the psyche, such as unbridled aggression, defensiveness, and the fight-or-flight response. It also represents the warrior archetype within us—the part that defends boundaries, fights for what it values, and pursues personal goals with determination. This archetype, when balanced, supports self-assertion and courage. When imbalanced, it can manifest as anger, recklessness, or burnout.

Mars is considered a malefic planet due to its association with inflammation, accidents, and excessive heat within the body and psyche. It governs the muscular system, motor nerves, and the production of adrenaline, influencing how we catalyze energy, handle stress, and assert ourselves in the world. However, when when someone is going through a hard-aspected Mars transit in a chart, or Mars' energy is excessive, it can lead to emotional upheaval, inflammation, high blood pressure, metabolic imbalance, and physical injuries such as fractures or muscle tears.

In mythology, Mars is personified by Ares, the Greek god of war, embodying the raw, unrefined aspects of conflict and power. Ares' narrative often illustrates the destructive potential of unchecked aggression, but also highlights the need

for courage and action. His fiery and impulsive nature reminds us that while passion and drive are essential for growth, they must be tempered with mindfulness and balance.

When to Use

Work with the energy of Mars when you need to summon courage, physical strength, and decisive action. Mars is particularly supportive during periods of inertia, self-doubt, or lack of direction, providing the energy and determination needed to overcome challenges and pursue goals.

This energy is also invaluable when navigating situations that require assertiveness, setting boundaries, or standing up for oneself. Mars strengthens resilience and promotes endurance, helping you persevere through adversity and emerge stronger. However, caution should be exercised when working with Mars energy during times of heightened stress, anger, or physical depletion, as it may exacerbate feelings of volatility or burnout.

Astrological Correspondences

Birth Chart

Mars Rules: Primarily associated with the Zodiac sign Aries, emphasizing themes of action and courage.

Exalted in Capricorn: Mars expresses disciplined and constructive energy, channeling its drive into long-term goals and achievements.

Detriment in Libra: Mars' assertive nature may struggle in Libra, where harmony and diplomacy are prioritized.

Organs

Muscular System: Governs physical strength and mobility.

Adrenal Glands: Influences adrenaline production, energy bursts, and the stress response.

Blood: Represents vitality, heat, and the circulation of energy.

Systems

Motor Nerves: Regulates action and movement.

Inflammatory Response: Oversees the body's defense mechanisms and reaction to injury or infection.

Hormonal Balance: Particularly linked to testosterone and other sex hormones.

Plants of *Mars*

Mars' planetary energy serves as a double-edged sword: it can propel us forward with strength and determination or overwhelm us with recklessness and anger. Herbs associated with Mars often share its fiery, invigorating qualities; however, their potent nature requires mindful use to avoid adverse effects. For instance, excess Mars energy can manifest as chronic inflammation, adrenal exhaustion, or emotional volatility. Learning to work with Mars energy involves channeling its intensity into productive and harmonious outlets.

Sweet Basil

(Ocimum basilicum)

Medicinal Properties Basil's warming and stimulating qualities align with Mars' energy. It aids digestion, reduces inflammation, and acts as an adaptogen, helping the body respond to stress. Basil is also known for its antimicrobial and immune-boosting properties, making it a powerful ally during periods of physical exertion or recovery.

Celestial Significance Sweet basil carries the energy of a protector and purifier, burning away negative influences and strengthening resilience. Its energy promotes mental clarity, focus, and resilience, helping individuals overcome obstacles and stay committed to their goals.

How to Use Herbal teas, infused oils, cooking, protection rituals, focus-enhancing meditation.

Caution Basil essential oil should be used sparingly and diluted, as excessive amounts can irritate the skin and mucus membranes.

Black Pepper

(Piper nigrum)

Medicinal Properties Black pepper is a powerful stimulant for the digestive and circulatory systems. Its warming nature enhances nutrient absorption and has mild prebiotic properties, supporting a balanced gut microbiome. Black pepper acts as a carminative, helping to reduce bloating and excessive gas in the digestive tract, and assists in detoxifying the liver and increasing bile flow. Additionally, its antioxidant properties protect against cellular damage and inflammation.

Celestial Significance Black pepper's warm and pungent nature resonates with Mars as it carries the fiery energy of initiation, making it a powerful ally in spells and rituals that require strength, resilience, and motivation. Just as Mars governs warriors and conflict, so black pepper acts as a catalyst for cutting through stagnation and pushing forward with determination. It stimulates the mind and body, promoting action, courage, and determination. Spiritually, it is used to banish negativity, energize intentions, and act as a psychic purifier, dissolving lower vibrations and shielding the aura from harmful influences.

How to Use Cooking, tinctures, circulatory stimulants, and energy-clearing rituals.

Caution Overuse may irritate the stomach lining or exacerbate acid reflux.

Cat's Claw

(Uncaria tomentosa)

Medicinal Properties Cat's claw has immune-boosting, anti-inflammatory, and antioxidant properties. It helps to regulate the immune system, making it beneficial for overall immune resilience. The herb also supports joint health, aids in post-exertion recovery, and helps combat chronic inflammation, oxidative stress, and digestive disorders. Additionally, it has been studied for its potential in supporting neurological health and cardiovascular function, offering broad-spectrum protection for the body.

Celestial Significance This herb aligns with Mars' healing and protective attributes, reinforcing the body's defenses and also accelerating recovery. Its thorny vines and deep-rooted strength symbolize resilience, endurance, and the ability to overcome adversity. As a plant of both protection and regeneration, cat's claw reflects the duality of Mars—the warrior who defends and the healer who restores. Spiritually, it is used for cleansing, shielding, and restoring balance after illness or emotional depletion.

How to Use Herbal teas, capsules, tinctures for immune support, joint health, inflammation reduction, and post-workout recovery. Can also be used in spiritual cleansing baths and protection rituals.

Caution Avoid use during pregnancy, while breastfeeding, or when taking immunosuppressive medications. The herb may interact with blood pressure and anticoagulant medications.

Cinnamon

(Cinnamomum verum)

Medicinal Properties Cinnamon's warming, stimulating, and balancing properties make it a rich herb for circulatory health, metabolic balance, and inflammation reduction. It helps stabilize blood sugar levels; its antimicrobial and antifungal qualities support immune health, while its ability to improve circulation aids in cardiovascular function and cognitive enhancement. Cinnamon is known to soothe digestion, reduce bloating, and combat infections.

Celestial Significance Cinnamon reflects the fiery essence of Mars, representing passion, vitality, courage, and drive. As a symbol of warmth and strength, it promotes motivation and determination, which makes it a powerful addition to manifestation rituals, success spells, and protective charms. It is widely used in money-drawing rituals, love spells, and for spiritual protection.

How to Use Infused oils, teas, cooking; money and abundance rituals, protection charms, love spells, and energy-boosting potions.

As a symbol of warmth and strength, cinnamon promotes motivation and determination.

Nettle

(Urtica dioica)

Medicinal Properties Nettle is a nutrient powerhouse, rich in iron, calcium, magnesium, and vitamins A, C, K, and B-complex, making it an excellent tonic for blood health, energy production, and immune support. It reduces inflammation, supports adrenal function, and helps the body recover from physical fatigue and stress. Nettle is also known for its diuretic and detoxifying properties, aiding in kidney function, liver health, and reducing water retention.

Celestial Significance Nettle has a protective and strengthening nature; just as its stinging leaves defend against harm, so too does it promote energetic boundaries, self-protection, and persistence. It is often used in rituals for strength, resilience, and overcoming obstacles, reinforcing both physical and spiritual fortitude.

How to Use Herbal infusions, tinctures, nourishing soups, energy-restoring tonics, protective amulets, stamina-boosting rituals, and spiritual baths.

Caution May interact with blood thinners, diuretics, and blood-pressure medications.

Nettle is often used in rituals for strength, resilience, and overcoming obstacles.

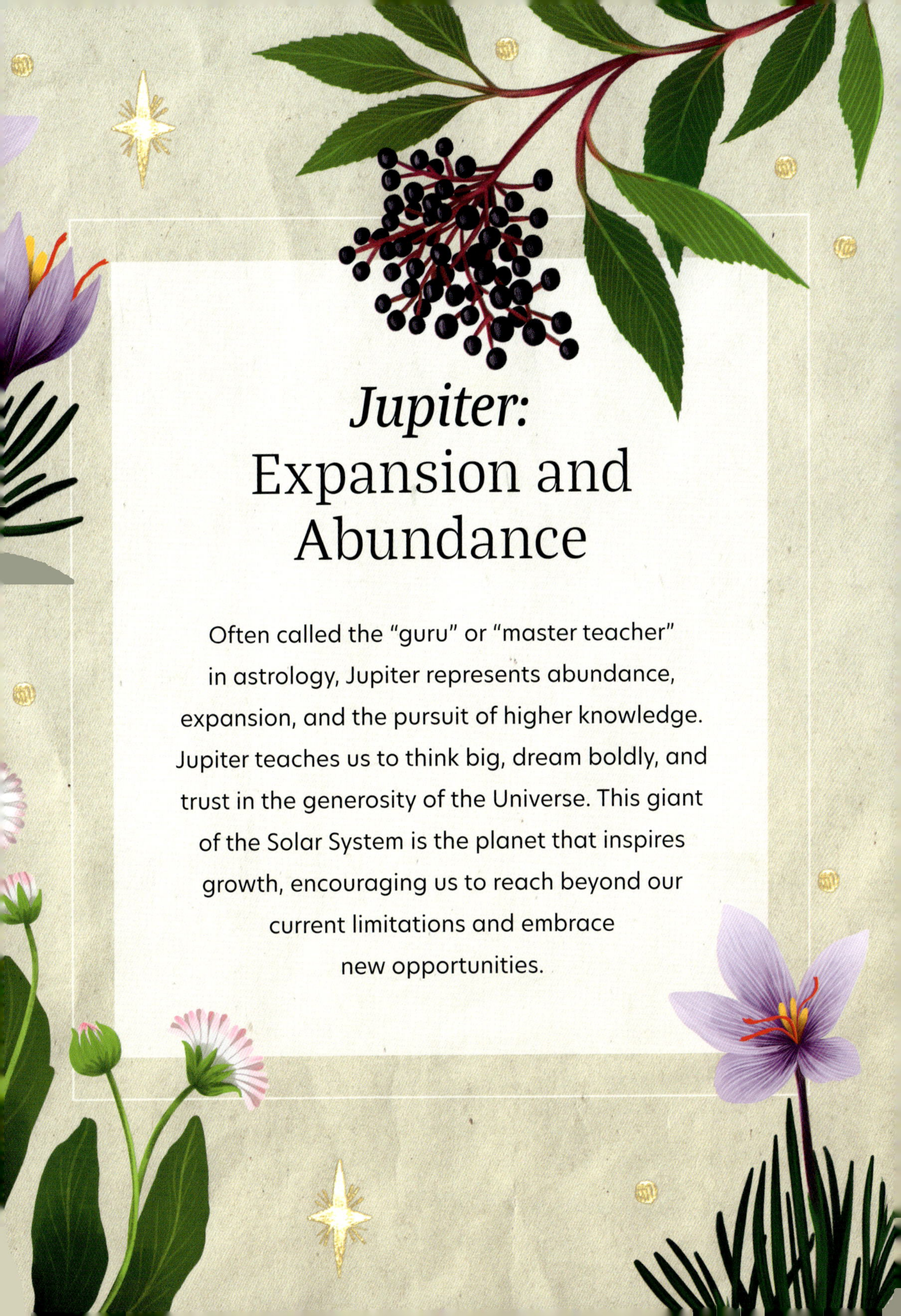

Jupiter: Expansion and Abundance

Often called the "guru" or "master teacher" in astrology, Jupiter represents abundance, expansion, and the pursuit of higher knowledge. Jupiter teaches us to think big, dream boldly, and trust in the generosity of the Universe. This giant of the Solar System is the planet that inspires growth, encouraging us to reach beyond our current limitations and embrace new opportunities.

♃ ♐

Archetypal Signature *of Jupiter*

In an astrological chart, Jupiter's position reveals how and where we seek growth, wisdom, and purpose. It highlights the areas of life where we are most likely to experience success and fulfillment, as well as the ways we approach learning and self-improvement. Jupiter's influence connects to optimism, faith, and the belief that life offers infinite possibilities.

Jupiter rules the signs of Sagittarius and Pisces, reflecting its dual nature as both the seeker of knowledge and the dreamer of spiritual truth. In Sagittarius, Jupiter represents exploration, philosophy, and adventure; it calls us to broaden our horizons through travel, education, and the pursuit of universal truths. In Pisces, Jupiter takes on a more mystical tone, guiding us toward creativity, compassion, and a deeper connection to the divine.

From a Jungian perspective, Jupiter represents the part of the psyche that expands—the aspect of ourselves that strives to grow beyond our current boundaries and reach for the unknown. This expansion often involves a quest for meaning, where we seek to understand the mysteries of life and our place within it. Jung emphasized the importance of individuation, a process of personal growth that requires integrating the conscious and unconscious parts of the self. Jupiter's energy supports this process by encouraging self-discovery, optimism, and the courage to face life's challenges with an open heart and mind.

Jupiter also reflects the teacher within us—the inner guide that helps us to navigate life's complexities and find purpose in our experiences. By tapping into Jupiter's energy, we can learn to trust in our own wisdom, find joy in the journey, and embrace the lessons that come our way. Expansion, however, is not just about material growth; it is also about inner growth. To expand in a meaningful way, we must cultivate self-awareness, gratitude, and a willingness to let go of limiting beliefs.

In Greek mythology Jupiter is associated with Zeus, the king of the gods who ruled with authority and wisdom. Zeus embodies power and generosity,

bestowing blessings upon those who align with their higher purpose. Like Zeus, Jupiter reminds us of the importance of balance—expansion must be tempered with wisdom and a sense of responsibility.

When to Use

The energy of Jupiter is best called upon when you are seeking growth, clarity, or a broader perspective. It is especially helpful when you feel stuck or limited in your thinking, helping to open the mind to new possibilities and opportunities. Use Jupiter's influence to inspire confidence, optimism, and a sense of faith in the bigger picture, particularly during times of uncertainty or when planning for long-term goals.

Jupiter's energy also supports rituals and practices focused on abundance and prosperity. It strengthens your ability to attract success and recognize opportunities for growth. For those on a spiritual journey, Jupiter can help to deepen your connection to wisdom and higher consciousness, offering insights into life's mysteries. This energy is also helpful when working to expand your horizons, whether through travel, education, or personal growth.

Astrological Correspondences

Birth chart

Jupiter Rules: Associated with Sagittarius, representing expansion, and wisdom.

Exalted in Cancer: Enhances Jupiter's nurturing and protective qualities, emphasizing abundance and emotional growth.

Detriment in Gemini and Virgo: Can bring challenges in balancing broad vision with attention to detail, leading to scattered energy or overthinking.

Organs

Liver: Governs detoxification and vitality, reflecting Jupiter's role in growth and renewal.

Lungs: Supports deep breathing and connection to expansive energy.

Systems

Digestive: Jupiter governs the digestive system, symbolizing the processing and assimilation of life's lessons.

Circulatory: Supports blood flow and the distribution of nutrients through the body, mirroring the planet's expansive and generous nature.

Plants *of Jupiter*

Herbs associated with Jupiter reflect its expansive and abundant energy. They support physical vitality, mental clarity, and spiritual growth, helping us to align with the planet's themes of success and prosperity. Jupiterian herbs like clove, daisy, elderberry, saffron crocus, and sweet violet are powerful allies for those seeking growth and fulfillment.

Clove

(Syzygium aromaticum)

Medicinal Properties Clove is a warming spice with antibacterial, antiviral, and pain-relieving properties; it supports digestion, helps relieve nausea, and can soothe respiratory discomfort. It is also a powerful antioxidant, protecting against oxidative stress and boosting immunity.

Celestial Significance Clove embodies Jupiter's expansive and warming energy, symbolizing abundance, protection, and spiritual growth. Traditionally, clove was used in rituals to attract prosperity and dispel negativity. Its stimulating qualities align with Jupiter's ability to inspire courage, confidence, and optimism. Clove's aromatic nature also creates clarity and focus, helping to align one's energy with success and abundance.

How to Use In teas or culinary dishes; use clove essential oil in diffusers or anointing rituals.

Caution Cloves may thin the blood, so they should be used with caution by individuals on anticoagulant medications or with bleeding disorders. Always speak with a medical practitioner before using if there are any potential contraindications.

Daisy

(*Bellis perennis*)

Medicinal Properties Daisy is a gentle herb used for its anti-inflammatory, detoxifying, and wound-healing properties. Daisy can also be used topically as a poultice or infused oil to soothe bruises, sprains, and minor injuries. It also supports the liver, kidneys, and lymphatic system, aiding the body in cleansing and renewal. Daisy also has a calming effect on the nervous system, helping to ease tension and promote relaxation.

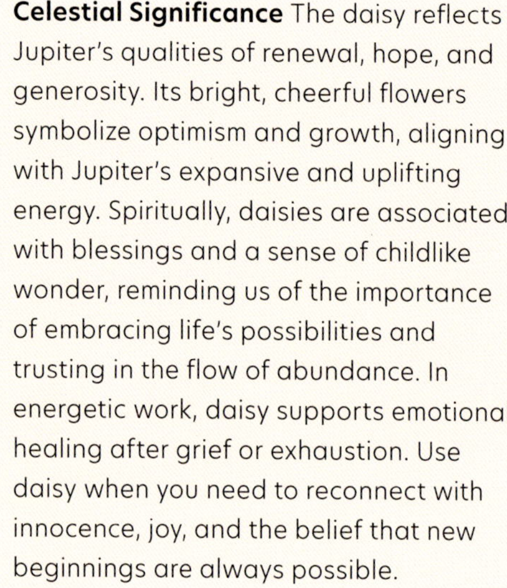

Celestial Significance The daisy reflects Jupiter's qualities of renewal, hope, and generosity. Its bright, cheerful flowers symbolize optimism and growth, aligning with Jupiter's expansive and uplifting energy. Spiritually, daisies are associated with blessings and a sense of childlike wonder, reminding us of the importance of embracing life's possibilities and trusting in the flow of abundance. In energetic work, daisy supports emotional healing after grief or exhaustion. Use daisy when you need to reconnect with innocence, joy, and the belief that new beginnings are always possible.

How to Use: Teas, tinctures, rituals for growth and renewal, as an altar offering.

Elderberry

(*Sambucus nigra*)

Medicinal Properties Elderberry, also known as the black elderberry or common elder, is widely recognized for its immune-boosting properties, making it a powerful ally against colds and flu. Rich in antioxidants, it supports the body's natural defences and promotes overall vitality. Elderberry is also beneficial for respiratory health, helping to ease congestion and soothe the throat.

Celestial Significance Elderberry reflects Jupiter's protective and abundant nature. It symbolizes resilience and vitality, offering both physical and spiritual protection. Elderberry's dark berries and lush growth connect it to themes of mystery, transformation, and the cycles of life, aligning with Jupiter's wisdom and expansive energy.

How to Use Take as a syrup, tea, or tincture; use in abundance rituals or as an offering to Jupiter.

Caution Elderberry may stimulate the immune system, so it should not be ingested by those with autoimmune conditions unless advised this is safe by a healthcare provider.

> Rich in antioxidants, elderberry supports the body's natural defences and promotes overall vitality.

Saffron Crocus

(*Crocus sativus*)

Medicinal Properties Saffron is prized for its uplifting and mood-enhancing properties, and has been traditionally used to alleviate symptoms of emotional instability. Its gentle action on the nervous system helps stabilize mood and promote emotional resilience without sedating or dulling the senses.

It also supports digestive health, stimulating appetite and easing symptoms of sluggish digestion or bloating. Its warming nature aids circulation, helping to move stagnant blood and support cardiovascular function, particularly in those prone to cold extremities or low energy.

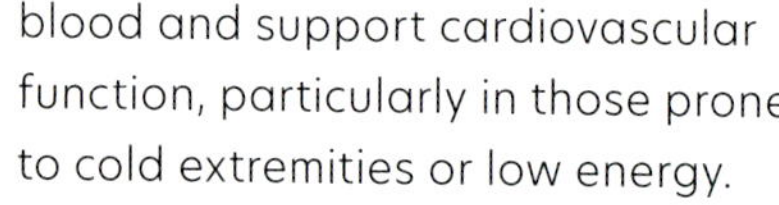

Saffron has antioxidant and anti-inflammatory properties, offering cellular protection and supporting long-term vitality. Because saffron is highly concentrated and potent, only a small amount is needed.

Celestial Significance Saffron embodies Jupiter's golden energy, symbolizing abundance, joy, and prosperity. It is often associated with spiritual enlightenment and celebration, reflecting Jupiter's role as a bringer of wisdom and success. The radiant color of saffron mirrors Jupiter's expansive and optimistic nature, inspiring creativity, positivity, and confidence.

How to Use Add to teas, broths, or culinary dishes; use in rituals or in meditation practices.

Sweet Violet

(Viola odorata)

Medicinal Properties Sweet violet is recognized for its anti-inflammatory and soothing properties. It supports respiratory health, eases congestion, and calms irritated skin. This much-loved garden flower also has a gentle effect on the nervous system, promoting relaxation and emotional balance.

Celestial Significance Sweet violet represents Jupiter's softer side, symbolizing peace, renewal, and inner abundance. The delicate flowers and subtle fragrance of the sweet violet reflect the planet's nurturing energy, encouraging introspection and emotional growth. Spiritually, sweet violet is associated with blessings, harmony, and alignment with higher truths.

How to Use Teas or infusions; use in beauty rituals, baths, and ceremonies.

Spiritually, sweet violet is associated with blessings, harmony, and alignment with higher truths.

Saturn: Discipline and Structure

This chapter explores the essence of order, growth, and perseverance as embodied by Saturn. We will explore how herbs such as arnica, barley, comfrey, cypress, and sacred fig promote Saturn's grounded and stabilizing energy, offering support for endurance, healing, and wisdom while reminding us of the hard but important lessons found in limitation.

♄ ♑

Archetypal Signature *of Saturn*

Saturn symbolizes the principles of discipline and responsibility, and the boundaries that define our lives. Often referred to as the taskmaster of the Zodiac, Saturn challenges us to grow through hard work, patience, and perseverance.

Saturn's energy is grounding and stabilizing, showing us the value of commitment, maturity, and accountability. Saturn also governs time, structure, and the material world, reminding us of the finite nature of existence and the importance of building strong foundations.

In the birth chart, Saturn reveals areas where we face limitations, fears, and lessons—but also where we can cultivate growth through persistence and effort. It represents the archetype of the wise elder, guiding us toward self-awareness and resilience through challenges. Saturn's influence or transits can feel heavy or restrictive sometimes, but it is through these challenges that we learn strength, integrity, and wisdom.

In Jungian psychology, Saturn can show the shadow aspects of the psyche that resist growth and transformation; it is the voice of doubt, fear, and rigidity, but also the force that pushes us toward self-discipline and responsibility. Saturn's shadow asks us to confront our fears of failure, inadequacy, and impermanence, encouraging us to integrate these aspects of ourselves and move forward with better self-understanding.

Like Mars (see pages 54–63), Saturn is sometimes considered a malefic planet due to its association with restriction, hardship, tests, and delays. However, these difficulties are often the very tools through which we grow and evolve.

Saturn governs the bones, joints, and connective tissues—the framework that supports our physical form and physical expansion. It also rules the processes of repair and recovery, chronic conditions, and aging.

The Roman god Saturn, or Cronus in Greek mythology, is associated with time, harvest, and inevitable change. The mythology of Saturn often highlights themes of mortality, the cycles of life and death, and the necessity of sacrifice.

While Cronus' story includes elements of tyranny and fear, it also teaches the importance of self-restraint and the rewards of diligent effort.

When to Use

Work the energy of Saturn when you need to cultivate discipline, perseverance, and resilience. Saturn is particularly supportive during times of recovery, structural instability (physical or emotional), or when you are trying to navigate life's challenges and responsibilities.

The planet's grounding energy is ideal for creating order out of chaos and fostering a sense of stability. Saturn's influence is also helpful when working with issues related to boundaries, aging, or chronic conditions. It encourages slow, deliberate healing and the establishment of sustainable practices.

Astrological Correspondences

Birth Chart

Saturn Rules: Primarily associated with the Zodiac sign of Capricorn, emphasizing themes of structure, discipline, and innovation within constraints.

Exalted in Libra: Saturn expresses its energy harmoniously in Libra, balancing discipline with fairness and beauty.

Detriment in Cancer: Saturn's restrictive nature can clash with Cancer's emotional sensitivity, leading to difficulties in emotional expression.

Organs

Bones: Representing structure, stability, and resilience.

Joints: Governing flexibility and mobility.

Skin: Serving as a boundary and protector of the body.

Systems

Skeletal System: Provides the framework for physical stability and endurance.

Connective Tissues: Ensures integrity and support throughout the body.

Repair Mechanisms: Governs processes of healing and recovery.

Plants *of* Saturn

Saturn's planetary energy invites us to look at life's challenges as opportunities for growth. The herbs aligned with Saturn often reflect its grounding, restorative, and protective qualities. These plants are known for their ability to support structural integrity, promote healing, and fortify the body against the effects of time and wear. However, working with Saturn energy also requires mindfulness, as its excess can lead to rigidity, stagnation, or feelings of heaviness and despair.

Arnica

(*Arnica montana*)

Medicinal Properties Arnica, also known as mountain arnica, is a powerful anti-inflammatory and pain-relieving herb, used for bruises, sprains, muscle soreness, and joint injuries. It helps to reduce swelling, accelerate tissue repair, and alleviate pain. It also supports circulatory health, improving blood flow to damaged areas, which aligns with its role in wound healing and reducing stiffness.

Celestial Significance Arnica has the endurance, discipline, and resilience of Saturn. It symbolizes slow but steady healing, reinforcing the necessity of patience and consistency in recovery. It is associated with overcoming obstacles, strengthening the will, and reinforcing boundaries, much like the protective nature of Saturn's rings.

How to Use Topical creams, infused oils, compresses for bruises, muscle pain, and joint injuries, and post-exercise recovery balms. Can also be used in rituals for resilience, grounding, and protection.

Caution Arnica should only be used topically, as internal consumption can be toxic. Avoid applying to broken skin, open wounds, or mucus membranes.

Barley

(Hordeum vulgare)

Medicinal Properties Barley is a nourishing and restorative grain that supports digestive health, metabolic balance, and overall vitality. Its high fiber content aids in cleansing the digestive tract, promoting gut health, and regulating blood sugar levels. Barley is rich in essential minerals like magnesium, phosphorus, and silicon, which help to strengthen the bones, connective tissues, and joints. Barley has cooling and soothing properties, making it beneficial for reducing inflammation and promoting hydration.

Celestial Significance Barley promotes the grounding, stabilizing, and enduring energy of Saturn. As an ancient staple grain, barley has long been associated with sustenance, longevity, and survival, making it a powerful spiritual ally in rituals for abundance, endurance, and protection against hardship. Its rooted energy also connects it to ancestral wisdom and traditions, reinforcing Saturn's ties to heritage, legacy, and karmic lessons.

How to Use Soups, porridges, teas, and ritual offerings for stability, endurance, and longevity. Also used in ancestral work and grounding rituals.

Barley has long been associated with sustenance, longevity, and survival.

Common comfrey

(Symphytum officinale)

Medicinal Properties Comfrey is a wound-healing and tissue-repairing herb, with its key compound, allantoin, promoting recovery from fractures, sprains, bruises, and joint injuries by stimulating new cell growth. It has a long history of use as a skin-healing agent, helping to treat burns, wounds, connective tissues, and ulcers.

Celestial Significance Comfrey embodies Saturn's grounding, restorative, and structuring energy. Just as Saturn rules bones, time, and endurance, so comfrey works slowly yet effectively to strengthen and rebuild the body's foundation. It symbolizes perseverance, stability, and recovery.

How to Use Poultices, salves, infused oils for external application, and compresses used for wounds, fractures, muscle pain, and joint issues. Also used in rituals for protection, endurance, and stability.

Caution Comfrey should not be taken orally as it can cause liver toxicity.

Comfrey works slowly yet effectively to strengthen and rebuild the body's foundation.

Italian Cypress

(*Cupressus sempervirens*)

Medicinal Properties Cypress is a circulatory stimulant and astringent, known for its ability to support blood flow, reduce fluid retention, and tone the vascular system. It is often used to improve circulation, relieve varicose veins, and ease muscle cramps or swelling. Its respiratory benefits make it effective for clearing congestion, soothing coughs, and strengthening lung function.

Celestial Significance Cypress embodies Saturn's role as a guardian through life's transitions and cycles, especially those related to transformation, endings, and grief. Often associated with mourning, ancestral connections, and spiritual endurance, cypress trees have long been planted in cemeteries as symbols of protection, longevity, and the eternal soul. This tree teaches acceptance of life's limitations, helping one find strength, wisdom, and stability during difficult times. It is also linked to perseverance, discipline, and purification.

> Cypress trees are planted as symbols of protection, longevity, and the eternal soul.

How to Use Essential oils for massage oils, aromatherapy, incense for grounding rituals, and spiritual purification practices.

Caution Cypress essential oil should be diluted before topical use and avoided during pregnancy. Individuals with sensitive skin or respiratory conditions should test for potential irritation before using.

Sacred Fig

(Ficus religiosa)

Medicinal Properties The sacred fig, revered in spiritual traditions, offers respiratory, anti-inflammatory, and calming benefits. Also known as the peepul tree, it is traditionally used to support lung health, alleviate asthma and coughs, and promote overall well-being. Rich in antioxidants and bioactive compounds, it helps to reduce oxidative stress, combat inflammation, and enhance immunity. The sacred fig is also valued for its nervous system-soothing properties, aiding in mental clarity, emotional balance, and stress reduction. Its calming effect on the mind reflects its role as a tree of wisdom and contemplation, making it an ally for meditative practices and cognitive focus.

Celestial Significance The sacred fig is a symbol of longevity, spiritual discipline, and deep introspection, mirroring Saturn's influence over karma, destiny, and inner growth. The bodhi tree, under which the Buddha attained enlightenment, is the most famous example of a sacred fig, further emphasizing the plant's associations with meditation, sacred knowledge, and enlightenment. It provides grounding energy, helping practitioners cultivate self-awareness, detachment, and resilience.

How to Use Spiritual offerings, altar adornments, sacred smoke rituals, wisdom-enhancing practices. Also used as a meditation aid. Can be planted for protection and divine connection.

Caution For ingestion, sacred fig preparations should be used under the guidance of a qualified practitioner to ensure proper usage and dosage.

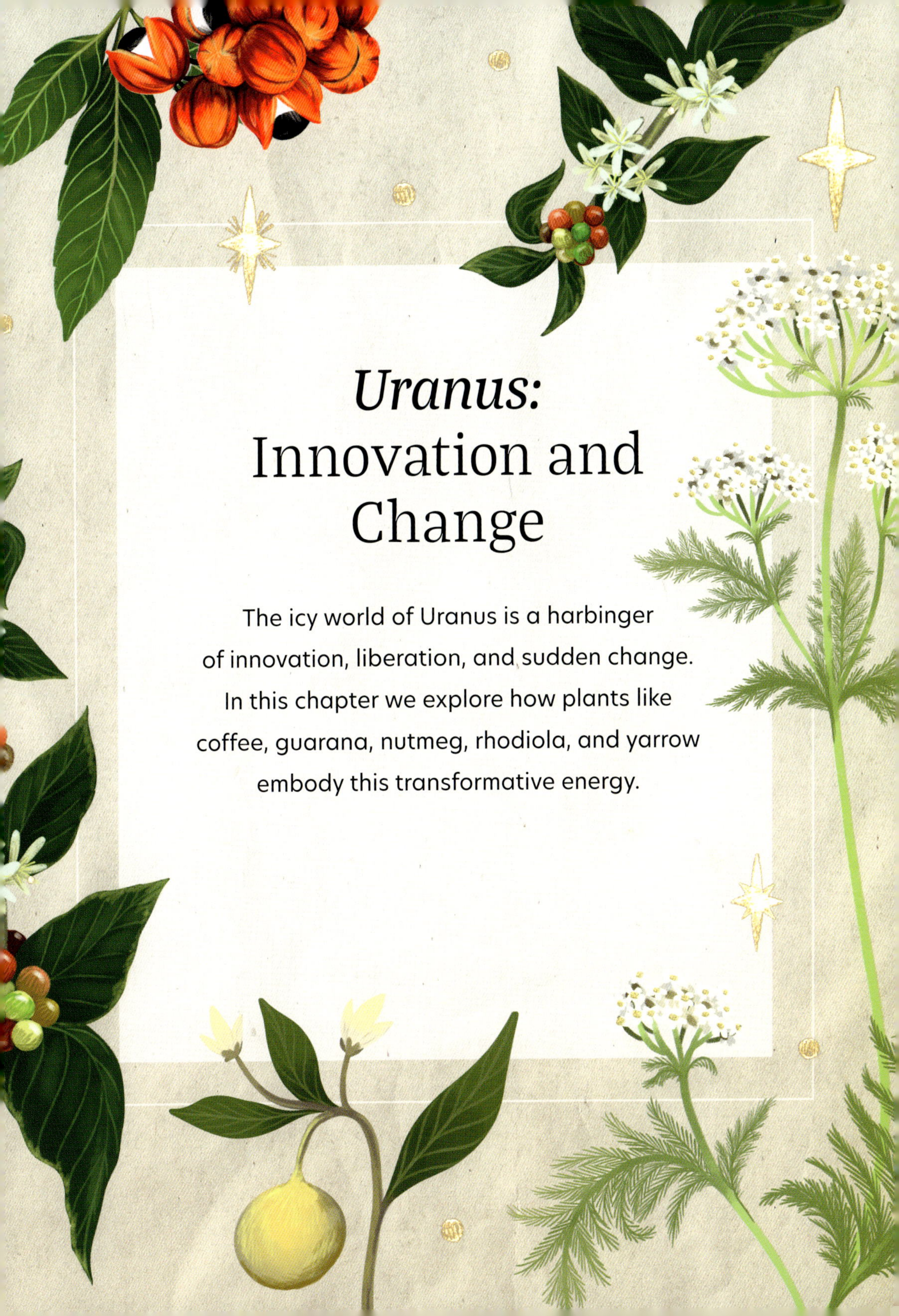

Uranus: Innovation and Change

The icy world of Uranus is a harbinger of innovation, liberation, and sudden change. In this chapter we explore how plants like coffee, guarana, nutmeg, rhodiola, and yarrow embody this transformative energy.

Archetypal Signature *of Uranus*

In astrology, Uranus symbolizes the principles of unpredictability, revolution, and originality. As the planet of sudden insight and change, Uranus shakes the foundations of established structures, inspiring freedom, innovation, and the courage to embrace the unconventional.

The planet's energy is disruptive yet enlightening, pushing us to transcend limitations and align with our authentic selves. In the birth chart, Uranus represents areas of life where we seek individuality and breakthroughs; it governs radical transformation, rebellion, and the capacity to envision and create a better future. Uranus' influence is often felt as flashes of insight or unexpected events that challenge our comfort zones, prompting growth and evolution.

Uranus can be associated with the archetype of the trickster or the genius—figures that disrupt the status quo to reveal hidden truths and open new possibilities. This archetype carries the creative spark of invention, the wisdom of chaos, and the capacity to bridge the gap between the known and the unknown.

Uranus is considered a neutral planet in astrology, with its malefic or benefic influence depending on how its energy is integrated. It governs the nervous system, electricity, and sudden surges of energy in both the body and the mind. While it inspires breakthroughs, excessive Uranian energy can lead to overstimulation, nervous tension, and some difficulty grounding oneself.

In mythology, Uranus is personified as the primordial sky god, representing limitless potential and the vast expanse of possibility. Uranus' mythological narrative highlights themes of creation, upheaval, and renewal—a reflection of its astrological energy.

When to Use

Work with the energy of Uranus when you need inspiration, a shift in perspective, or creative problem-solving. Uranus is especially potent during collective shifts, social movements, or personal awakenings, when old systems no longer serve and new paradigms are emerging. Its energy favours experimentation,

visionary thinking, and sudden alignment with your inner truth. Uranus is supportive during times of stagnation or when navigating transitions that require adaptability and resilience. The planet's power enhances mental clarity, intuition, and the ability to see beyond conventional boundaries. This energy is also helpful when seeking liberation from outdated habits, beliefs, or structures. Uranus encourages breaking free from conformity and embracing individuality.

When used intentionally, Uranus can help you access unconventional solutions, disrupt fear-based patterns, and reconnect with your most authentic direction. It is a planetary ally for innovators, healers, outsiders, and those daring enough to question norms and imagine a radically different future.

Astrological Correspondences

Birth Chart

Uranus Rules: Primarily associated with the Zodiac sign Aquarius and its themes of innovation, freedom, and collective progress.

Exalted in Scorpio: Uranus' energy is amplified in Scorpio, deepening its power to provoke change and rebirth.

Detriment in Leo: Uranus may struggle in Leo, where individuality clashes with the need for recognition and authority.

Organs

Brain: Governing intellectual activity and innovation.

Nervous System: Regulating electrical impulses and responses to change.

Circulation: Representing the flow of energy and vitality.

Systems

Nervous System: Governing adaptation and the transmission of signals.

Electrical Impulses: These reflect sudden shifts and surges of energy.

Cognitive Function: Enhancing clarity, focus, and higher awareness.

Plants *of* Uranus

Herbs associated with Uranus often share its stimulating and adaptive qualities, promoting alertness, resilience, and clarity. However, these potent plants must be used mindfully, as their energy can overwhelm or destabilize when taken in excess.

Arabian Coffee

(*Coffea arabica*)

Medicinal Properties Arabian coffee is a potent nervous system stimulant, enhancing mental alertness, cognitive function, and physical energy. Coffee also acts as a natural digestive aid, stimulating gastric juices and promoting healthy bowel movements. As a diuretic, it helps eliminate excess water and supports kidney function. Additionally, coffee is rich in antioxidants, helping to combat oxidative stress, protect cells from damage, and reduce the risk of neurodegenerative diseases.

Celestial Significance Coffee embodies Uranus' electrifying and revolutionary energy, stimulating rapid thought, heightened perception, and bursts of inspiration. Coffee also carries a rebellious and disruptive energy, much like Uranus, helping to break stagnant patterns and push beyond limitations. Spiritually, it can be used to recharge energy, increase awareness, and strengthen intention during manifestation rituals.

How to Use Brewed coffee, tinctures, energy-boosting rituals, mental clarity spells, and creative work enhancements.

Caution: Excessive consumption may cause jitters, anxiety, or insomnia.

Guarana

(*Paullinia cupana*)

Medicinal Properties Guarana is a potent natural stimulant, known for its high caffeine content, which provides a sustained energy boost, enhanced mental focus, and improved physical endurance. Unlike coffee, guarana releases caffeine slowly, offering long-lasting alertness without a sudden crash. It supports cognitive function, mood elevation, and motivation, making it beneficial for mental clarity and productivity. It has antioxidant and anti-inflammatory properties that guard against oxidative stress and cellular damage, contributing to overall longevity and vitality.

Celestial Significance Guarana embodies Uranus' electrifying, unpredictable, and forward-moving energy, fueling bold exploration, innovation, and adaptability. As a plant that provides bursts of energy and heightened mental clarity, it aligns with Uranus' role as the awakener, helping to break through mental and physical stagnation.

How to Use Energy drinks, teas, supplements, rituals for focus, stamina, and new ventures. Can also be used in manifestation work and intention-setting practices in order to amplify drive and determination.

Guarana provides bursts of energy and heightened mental clarity.

Nutmeg

(Myristica fragrans)

Medicinal Properties Nutmeg is a balancing herb for the nervous system, known for its calming and mildly sedative effects. The herb supports relaxation, stress relief, and improved sleep quality; it also aids digestion, helping to soothe bloating, nausea, and indigestion while stimulating appetite and digestive enzymes. Nutmeg contains anti-inflammatory and antioxidant compounds, helping to combat oxidative stress and neurodegenerative conditions.

Celestial Significance Nutmeg embodies Uranus' paradoxical energy, oscillating between stimulation and deep relaxation. It is an herb of insight and transformation, often used in visionary work, divination, and rituals for mental expansion. Nutmeg's dual nature allows it to be both a catalyst for innovation and a remedy for nervous exhaustion, helping to stabilize the rapid shifts Uranus brings.

How to Use Culinary spice, teas, and tinctures. Can also be used as an aromatic incense for grounding rituals, divination, and mental clarity.

Caution: Large doses of nutmeg can be toxic, leading to adverse effects on the nervous system. It should be used in moderation, especially for those with a sensitivity to stimulants. Avoid in pregnancy.

> An herb of insight and transformation, nutmeg is often used in visionary work.

Rhodiola

(Rhodiola rosea)

Medicinal Properties Rhodiola, also known as roseroot, is a powerful adaptogen, meaning that it enhances the body's ability to cope with stress, fatigue, and mental strain. Also known as rose root, the herb supports physical endurance, cognitive function, and emotional resilience, making it an excellent choice for those experiencing burnout, anxiety, or high mental demands. Rhodiola is known to reduce cortisol levels, helping to balance stress responses without causing sedation or overstimulation.

Celestial Significance Rhodiola offers strength and clarity amid chaos, reflecting Uranus' energy by helping individuals thrive in unpredictable circumstances. In much the same way that Uranus brings revolution and new perspectives, so rhodiola stimulates mental agility, innovation, and the ability to push beyond your limitations.

How to Use Capsules, tinctures, teas, and elixirs for focus, energy, and stress resilience.

> Rhodiola is known to reduce cortisol levels, helping to balance stress responses.

Yarrow

(Achillea millefolium)

Medicinal Properties Yarrow is a potent healer, known for its ability to stem bleeding, accelerate wound healing, and reduce inflammation. It is used to support circulation, regulate blood pressure, and improve overall vascular health. Yarrow also has antimicrobial and astringent properties, making it valuable for cleansing wounds, soothing digestive issues, and easing menstrual discomfort. It has a calming effect on the nervous system, helping to reduce stress, anxiety, and emotional turmoil, meaning that it is an essential herb for emotional and physical recovery.

Celestial Significance Yarrow reflects Uranus' role as a healer and protector, offering clarity, strength, and resilience during times of upheaval. It is often used in protective and visionary work, enabling individuals to navigate uncertainty with confidence and wisdom.

How to Use Herbal teas, tinctures, ritual baths for protection, resilience, and emotional balance, and spiritual work for insight and adaptation.

Caution: Yarrow may cause allergic reactions in individuals sensitive to plants in the Asteraceae family (such as chamomile or ragweed). Avoid during pregnancy.

> Yarrow has a calming effect on the nervous system, helping to reduce emotional turmoil.

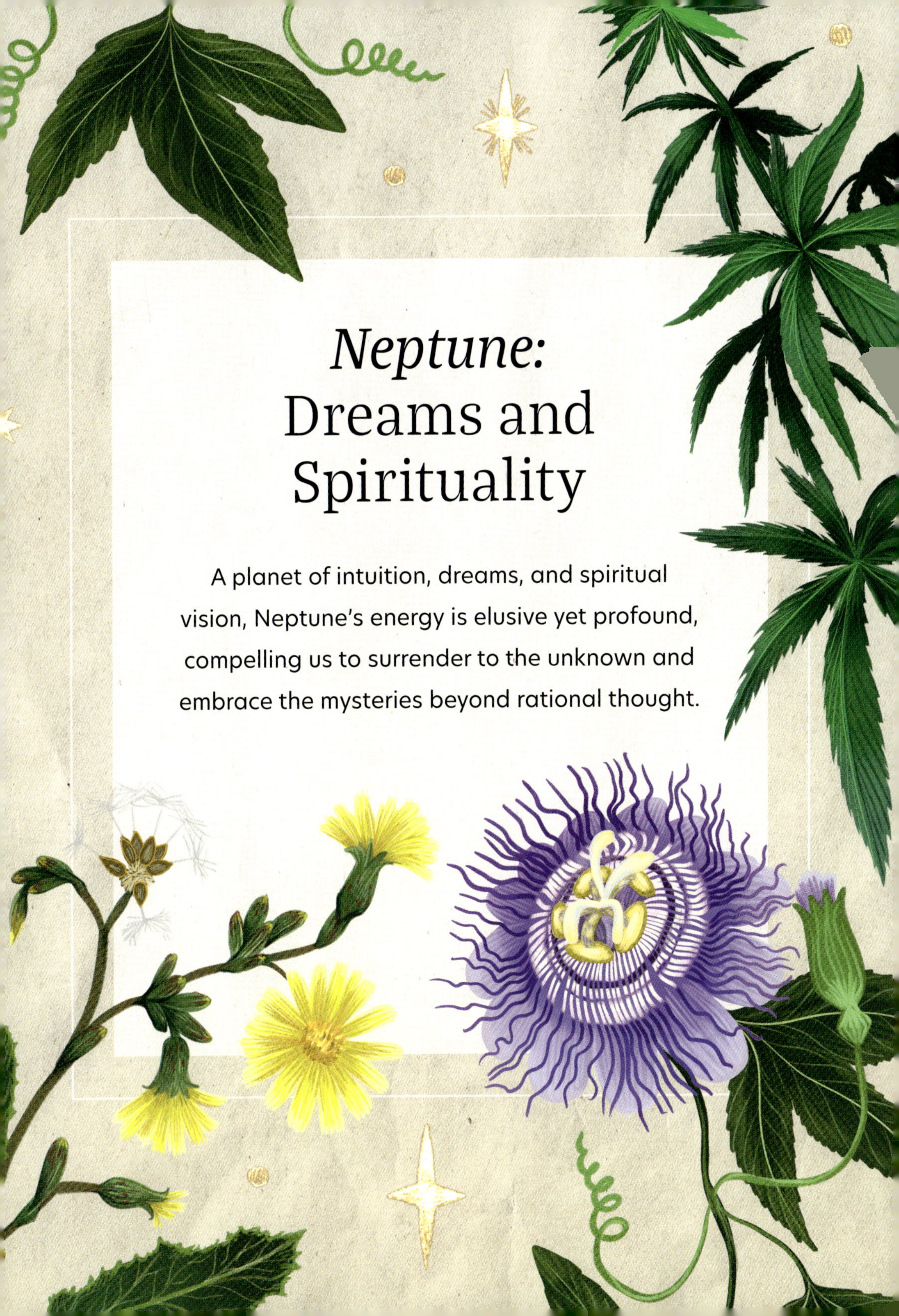

Neptune: Dreams and Spirituality

A planet of intuition, dreams, and spiritual vision, Neptune's energy is elusive yet profound, compelling us to surrender to the unknown and embrace the mysteries beyond rational thought.

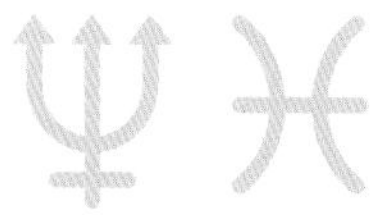

Archetypal Signature *of Neptune*

In astrology, Neptune symbolizes the principle of mysticism, imagination, and dissolution of boundaries. As the planet of dreams and intuition, Neptune removes the structures of ordinary perception, opening the mind to higher consciousness, spiritual insight, and artistic inspiration.

In the birth chart, Neptune represents the areas of life in which we seek transcendence, creativity, and spiritual connection. It governs fantasy, illusion, and the capacity to dream beyond material limitations. Neptune's influence is often felt as heightened intuition, deep emotional sensitivity, or a yearning to merge with something greater than oneself—whether that is a cause, a community, or the Universe.

Neptune can be associated with the archetype of the mystic, the artist, or the dreamer—figures that dissolve reality to reveal hidden dimensions and deeper truths. This archetype embodies the beauty of vision, the wisdom of surrender, and the ability to channel inspiration from the unseen realms.

Neptune is considered a neutral planet in astrology, its influence being either enlightening or confusing, depending on how its energy is integrated. It governs the pineal gland, dreams, and the flow of subconscious impressions. While it fosters spiritual insight, excessive Neptunian energy can lead to escapism, addiction, illusion, or emotional overwhelm.

In mythology, Neptune is personified as the god of the sea, ruling over the vast, shifting tides of emotion and perception. His mythological narrative focuses on themes of flow, surrender, and the cyclical nature of reality—a reflection of his astrological energy.

When to Use

Work with the energy of Neptune when you need to access inspiration or heightened spiritual awareness. This energy is also particularly supportive during times of meditation and creative endeavors. It enhances intuition, emotional depth, and the ability to access subconscious wisdom. This energy is also

helpful when seeking a connection to the divine. Neptune encourages dissolving rigid perceptions and accepting the fluid nature of identity, meaning, and emotion. It softens control, helps us trust in unseen guidance, and surrender to the rhythms of intuition and feeling.

Neptune can support inner work related to forgiveness, compassion, and spiritual healing, helping you release the ego's grip and reconnect with a deeper sense of unity. Its influence is ideal for exploring symbols, archetypes, and dreams, especially when words fall short and understanding must come through image, sensation, or inner knowing.

Astrological Correspondences

Birth chart

Neptune Rules: Associated with Pisces and its themes of spirituality, imagination, and dissolution.

Exalted in Leo: Neptune's energy is magnified in Leo, enhancing visionary creativity and divine inspiration.

Detriment in Virgo: Neptune may struggle in Virgo, where its fluid nature clashes with the need for order and logic.

Organs

Pineal Gland: Governing dream activity and intuitive perception.

Lymphatic System: Representing purification and fluid movement.

Feet: Symbolizing the connection to the subconscious and spiritual realms.

Systems

Endocrine: Governing hormonal flow and altered states of consciousness.

Psychic Sensory Perception: Enhancing intuition and spiritual receptivity.

Sleep Cycles: Regulating dream activity and subconscious insights.

Plants of *Neptune*

Herbs associated with Neptune often share its calming, hypnotic, and expansive qualities, promoting relaxation, dreamwork, and deep intuition. However, these plants must be used mindfully, as their effects can blur the line between reality and illusion.

Blue Lotus

(Nymphaea caerulea)

Medicinal Properties Blue lotus, also known as Egyptian lotus, is a mild euphoric and relaxant, known for its ability to induce deep relaxation, enhance dream recall, and promote spiritual insight. It supports emotional balance, helping to alleviate stress and anxiety. Blue lotus also has aphrodisiac and circulatory benefits.

Celestial Significance Blue lotus reflects Neptune's mystical and visionary energy, expanding consciousness and deepening dream experiences. It serves as a bridge between the material and the spiritual, aiding in meditation, divination, and lucid dreaming. Blue lotus is known for enhancing the ability to receive symbolic messages through dreams, making it a potent ally for those working with dream interpretation, astral travel, or accessing subconscious wisdom. Many traditions consider the blue lotus to be a sacred plant for its role in spiritual transformation, connecting the user to intuition, inspiration, and inner peace.

How to Use Teas, tinctures, and incense for dreamwork, relaxation, and spiritual ceremonies.

Caution In high doses, blue lotus may cause drowsiness and should be avoided before activities requiring full alertness, such as driving. Pregnant and breastfeeding should consult a healthcare provider before use.

Hemp

(Cannabis sativa)

Medicinal Properties Hemp is a deeply versatile and adaptive plant, known for its ability to balance the nervous system, reduce inflammation, and promote relaxation without sedation. It regulates mood, stress response, sleep, and immune function. CBD-dominant strains provide neuroprotective, anti-inflammatory, and calming benefits, making them an ideal remedy for stress, anxiety, chronic pain, and sleep disturbances. THC-rich varieties can induce euphoria, altered perception, and deep introspection, enhancing creativity and sensory awareness. While its effects can be profoundly soothing, high doses of THC may cause paranoia, dissociation, or overstimulation. Proper dosing and mindful use are essential to harness this plant's full potential.

Celestial Significance Hemp mirrors Neptune's fluid, boundary-dissolving, and visionary nature, enhancing dreamwork, artistic expression, and spiritual introspection. It facilitates altered states of consciousness, dissolves ego-driven anxieties, and opens the mind to higher dimensions of thought. Much like Neptune's dual influence, hemp can either deepen awareness or create escapism, depending on its use.

How to Use CBD oils, tinctures, and teas for relaxation, pain relief, and emotional balance; topical applications for pain and inflammation relief.

Caution Only for use by adults. Not suitable for individuals prone to psychosis or schizophrenia as it may exacerbate symptoms. High doses of THC may induce paranoia, anxiety, or mental fog—always consult a medical practitioner and start with low amounts. Legal status varies globally; ensure compliance with local regulations. Hemp may interact with sedatives, antidepressants, and blood pressure medications. Avoid during pregnancy and breastfeeding.

Marshmallow

(Althaea officinalis)

Medicinal Properties Marshmallow is a deeply soothing and protective herb, renowned for its ability to coat and heal irritated tissues. Its rich mucilage content forms a protective layer over the respiratory, digestive, and urinary tracts, offering relief for acid reflux, dry coughs, sore throats, and digestive discomfort. Beyond its physical healing abilities, marshmallow has a calming effect on the nervous system, promoting emotional healing, inner peace, and gentle relaxation. It acts as a mood stabilizer, helping to alleviate grief, emotional overwhelm, and psychic exhaustion.

Celestial Significance Marshmallow teaches acceptance, allowing one to flow through emotions rather than resist them. Used in dreamwork or spiritual practices, it can enhance connection to the subconscious while providing a sense of protection from external chaos. Its watery energy makes it a powerful ally during times of transition, loss, or emotional healing, allowing for graceful surrender and renewal.

How to Use Teas, infusions, and topical applications.

Caution May slow the absorption of medications; take separately from prescriptions. Avoid in cases of severe water retention or kidney issues, as it promotes fluid retention.

Marshamallow can enhance connection to the subconscious while providing a sense of protection from external chaos.

Purple Passionflower

(*Passiflora incarnata*)

Medicinal Properties Purple passionflower, also known as apricot vine, is a potent anxiolytic, hypnotic, and nerve relaxant, known for its ability to quiet mental chatter, ease tension, and promote deep sleep. It works by increasing GABA levels in the brain, which helps to reduce anxiety and nervous overstimulation. This herb is particularly beneficial for relieving insomnia, circular thinking, emotional agitation, and stress-related headaches. Unlike stronger sedatives, passionflower gently induces relaxation without causing drowsiness.

Celestial Significance Passionflower acts as a gateway to dreamlike consciousness, enhancing lucid dreaming, intuitive downloads, and meditation. Like Neptune's oceanic influence, passionflower teaches surrender and trust in the unknown, helping individuals to move through spiritual awakening and emotional release with grace. It is a particularly powerful herb for those who are struggling with mental overactivity, sleep disturbances, or difficulty relinquishing control.

How to Use Herbal teas, tinctures, extracts, and capsules.

Caution May enhance the effects of sedatives and antidepressants. Can cause drowsiness in some individuals and should be avoided before driving or operating machinery. Not recommended during pregnancy as it may induce uterine contractions.

Wild Lettuce

(Lactuca virosa)

Medicinal Properties Wild lettuce—also known as bitter lettuce—is a powerful sedative, pain reliever, and hypnotic herb, often used for insomnia, nervous restlessness, and tension headaches. It contains lactucarium, a compound with mild (non-addictive) opiate-like properties, which promotes deep relaxation and heightened dream activity. It is particularly useful for those who experience racing thoughts, restless sleep, or difficulty accessing dream states. In larger doses, it can induce a mild euphoric or trance-like state, making it a valuable tool for deep introspection, vision quests, and meditation.

Celestial Significance Wild lettuce aligns with Neptune's gateway to altered consciousness, helping individuals to dissolve barriers between waking and dream states. It enhances dream recall, deepens meditation, and supports astral exploration. Wild lettuce can either open doorways to insight or create a sense of detachment and confusion, depending on dosage and intent.

How to Use Teas and tinctures.

Caution Can cause extreme drowsiness and should not be combined with sedatives. May lead to dizziness or mild hallucinations in high doses. Not recommended for those with low blood pressure or liver issues. Avoid during pregnancy and breastfeeding.

Pluto: Transformation and Regeneration

A celestial body of transformation, death, and rebirth, Pluto possesses a potent and mysterious energy. In this chapter we will explore how herbs like black walnut, dragon's blood, and blue skullcap encapsulate Pluto's essence of deep healing, purification, and renewal.

Archetypal Signature *of Pluto*

Far out in the Solar System, in the distant Kuiper Belt, the enigmatic dwarf planet Pluto governs the cycles of destruction and rebirth, power dynamics, and the deepest realms of the subconscious mind. As a force of radical transformation, Pluto reveals hidden truths, stripping away illusions and forcing confrontation with what is often feared or repressed. Pluto does not negotiate change—it demands it, often through cathartic experiences that leave nothing as it was before.

In the birth chart, Pluto signifies times at which we must undergo profound metamorphosis, power struggles, and experiences of deep psychological transformation. It rules over themes of control, survival instincts, karmic lessons, and the unconscious drives that shape behavior. Wherever Pluto is found within the chart, it brings intensity, depth, and a need for complete surrender to evolution. This planet governs the mysteries of life and death, and the capacity to rise stronger from adversity.

Pluto's lessons often manifest through crises, revealing where we must let go of old identities, attachments, and fears. It governs shadow work, helping individuals to integrate their unconscious selves and break free from destructive cycles. As the ruler of Scorpio, Pluto thrives in depth, uncovering psychological wounds, buried desires, and latent potential.

Pluto's connection to power is twofold—on the one hand, it represents control, dominance, and the darker aspects of manipulation and coercion. On the other hand, it symbolizes true empowerment: the ability to reclaim inner strength by surrendering to necessary change. Those who embrace Pluto's energy learn to wield their personal power wisely, developing the resilience to navigate life's most difficult transformations.

In mythology, Pluto (known as Hades in Greek tradition) is the ruler of the Underworld, guardian of hidden wealth, and master of the unseen. His domain is not only the land of the dead but also the source of immense subterranean riches—symbolizing the buried potential that emerges through deep inner work.

Pluto's mythological role underlines themes of descent, initiation, and the ultimate rebirth that follows surrendering to life's inevitable transformations.

Plutonian energy is not gentle, but it is profoundly necessary. It governs the processes of cellular regeneration, detoxification, and emotional healing at the deepest levels. While its force may feel destructive, it ultimately clears the way for new growth, ensuring that what remains is purified and strengthened.

When to Use

The energy of Pluto is a powerful aide for those undergoing deep personal transformation, shadow work, or emotional and physical healing. Pluto's influence is supportive during times of crisis, loss, or major life changes, helping you to navigate transitions with strength and clarity.

Pluto's energy is also beneficial for overcoming trauma, breaking destructive patterns, and accessing deep spiritual insight. It assists in detoxification, empowerment, and working through subconscious fears or past-life influences.

Astrological Correspondences

Birth chart

Pluto Rules: Primarily associated with Scorpio, governing themes of power, depth, and transformation.

Exalted in Aries: Pluto's transformative energy is strengthened in Aries, driving forceful regeneration and rebirth.

Detriment in Taurus: Pluto struggles in Taurus, where its demand for change conflicts with stability and resistance to upheaval.

Organs

Reproductive System: Governing cycles of creation, destruction, and rebirth.

Excretory System: Supporting detoxification and purification.

Cellular Regeneration: Facilitating deep healing and renewal.

Systems

Detoxification: Governing the elimination of toxins, both physical and emotional.

Subconscious Mind: Unveiling hidden truths and facilitating transformation.

Endocrine: Regulating deep, transformative hormonal changes.

Plants *of* Pluto

Herbs associated with Pluto often possess intense medicinal and energetic properties. Many are toxic or psychoactive, requiring careful use and respect. These plants act as catalysts for deep healing, breaking through stagnation, purging impurities, and guiding transformation on both physical and spiritual levels.

Black Walnut

(*Juglans nigra*)

Medicinal Properties Black walnut is a powerful antifungal, antiparasitic, and detoxifying herb. Its high tannin content makes it effective for purging parasites, eliminating infections, and promoting digestive health. It is used to treat fungal infections such as candida, expel intestinal parasites, and cleanse metabolic waste. The green hulls of black walnut are especially potent in removing stagnation from the body and assisting in liver detoxification. It is also used to treat skin conditions such as eczema and psoriasis.

Celestial Significance Black walnut reflects Pluto's purgative and protective nature, clearing away toxicity, stagnation, and energetic blockages. It is a plant of strength, resilience, and protection, often used in banishing rituals and personal empowerment spells. It can also be used to break unhealthy attachments, helping individuals to sever ties to toxic influences and reclaim their power.

How to Use Tinctures, teas, and external applications for cleansing and protection.

Caution Strong detoxifier; use in moderation to avoid excessive purging effects.

Dragon's Blood

(*Daemonorops draco*)

Medicinal Properties Dragon's blood is a potent wound healer, astringent, and immune booster. It is highly effective for treating ulcers, reducing inflammation, and accelerating tissue regeneration. Used in traditional medicine for its antimicrobial, antiviral, and pain-relieving properties, it aids in blood purification

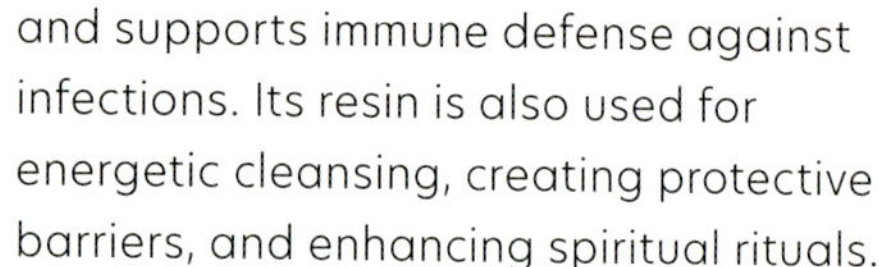

and supports immune defense against infections. Its resin is also used for energetic cleansing, creating protective barriers, and enhancing spiritual rituals.

Celestial Significance Associated with Pluto's raw power, dragon's blood represents sacrifice, transformation, and strength. It is widely used in magical practices for sealing spells, strengthening intentions, and amplifying energy. It aids in protection rituals, banishing negativity, and reinforcing personal power.

How to Use Resin for incense, tinctures, or topical applications.

Caution Use externally with care; internal use should always be guided by an experienced herbalist.

Dragon's blood aids in protection rituals, banishing negativity, and reinforcing personal power.

Blue Skullcap

(Scutellaria lateriflora)

Medicinal Properties Blue skullcap is a deeply restorative nervine, known for its ability to calm the nervous system, reduce anxiety, and promote restful sleep. It is beneficial for those experiencing chronic stress, nervous exhaustion, or trauma. Skullcap also has anti-inflammatory and antioxidant properties, making it supportive of brain health and cognitive function. It helps to balance mood swings and is commonly used for insomnia, nightmares, and emotional distress.

Celestial Significance Skullcap has a force of deep healing and renewal. It aids in emotional detoxification, helping individuals to release subconscious fears and anxieties. This herb is used in ritual work to enhance spiritual resilience, aid in letting go of past wounds, and strengthen psychic boundaries. It is particularly valuable in grief work, allowing for gentle emotional processing and an acceptance of transformation.

How to Use Teas, tinctures, and herbal baths for emotional balance, relaxation, and spiritual grounding.

Caution May cause drowsiness; avoid combining with sedatives.

> Skullcap helps individuals to release subconscious fears and anxieties.

Astro Herbalism in Practice

Astro Herbalism is not merely a theory—it is a living, breathing practice that allows us to integrate planetary energies into our daily lives. The formulas in this chapter will enable you to harness the powerful energy of the Zodiac through herbal applications.

Rituals and Recipes

In the previous chapters we have discovered that each celestial body governs specific aspects of everyday life, and that by working with their corresponding plants we create a harmonious bridge between cosmic rhythms and the natural world.

This chapter provides practical recipes and rituals that allow you to directly engage with planetary energies, whether through teas, tinctures, baths, oils, incense, or spiritual talismans. Each formulation is designed to align with the planet's core essence, helping you to embody and work with its influence in a meaningful way.

The suggested remedies are meant to be both practical and mystical, offering tools for physical well-being, energetic alignment, and spiritual growth. However, there are many ways to use each plant, and you can experiment to create personalized herbal remedies that work for you. Suggestions on ways to use each plant are given in the previous chapters.

The effectiveness of astro-herbal applications is significantly influenced by timing, intention, and alignment with natural cycles. Consider the following when working with planetary energies:

Planetary Days

Planetary days are an ancient system used in both magical and medicinal practices, where each day of the week is ruled by a specific celestial body. Aligning your herbal preparations, rituals, and personal work with these days strengthens their effects:

Sunday (Sun)
Best for vitality, confidence, success, and personal empowerment. Solar herbs are used in teas, infused oils, and incense to boost energy and radiance (see page 14).

Monday (Moon)
Supports intuition, dreamwork, emotional balance, and subconscious exploration. Lunar herbs are often used in teas, sleep sachets, and anointing oils (see page 24).

Tuesday (Mars)
Enhances courage, strength, endurance, and protection. Mars-related formulas include stimulating tonics, muscle rubs, and fiery incense for assertiveness (see page 54).

Wednesday (Mercury)

Aids mental clarity, communication, learning, and travel. Mercury herbs are best prepared in teas, elixirs, and incense to enhance focus and articulation (see page 34).

Thursday (Jupiter)

Expands wisdom, prosperity, and luck. Jupiterian herbs work well in anointing oils, growth-promoting teas, and abundance-enhancing baths (see page 64).

Friday (Venus)

Strengthens love, beauty, harmony, and sensuality. Venus herbs are often used in floral teas, perfumes, and self-care baths to invoke attraction and pleasure (see page 44).

Saturday (Saturn)

Supports discipline, grounding, protection, and long-term stability. Saturnian herbs are frequently found in boundary-setting oils, bone-strengthening teas, and banishing incenses (see page 74).

Neptune, and Pluto don't have traditional weekday rulerships, but their energies can be worked with on any day, depending on your intention.

Lunar Phases

The moon cycle plays a key role in herbal preparation, affecting how plants interact with our bodies, minds, and spiritual practices. Some formulas work best when made or used under specific lunar phases, depending on their purpose:

New Moon ●

Best for setting intentions, planting seeds for new projects, and initiating healing journeys. Saturn, Mercury, and Neptune formulas are particularly potent during this time.

Waxing Moon ☽

Encourages growth, attraction, and building energy. This is a prime time for Venus, Jupiter, and Sun remedies that promote beauty, expansion, and success.

Full Moon ○

Amplifies energy, heightens intuition, and reveals clarity. Lunar and Neptunian formulas, especially dream teas, spiritual baths, and psychic mists, are most effective here.

Waning Moon ☾

A time for release, purification, and introspection. Mars, Uranus, Pluto, and Saturn formulas—especially protection rituals, detoxifying teas, and shadow work incenses—are well suited to this moon phase.

The Sun: Vitality and Energy

Golden Vitality Tea

An infusion that awakens inner fire, strengthens immunity, and enhances personal power.

Ingredients:

- 1 cup hot water
- 1 tsp dried turmeric (or ½ tsp fresh, grated)
- 1 tsp dried calendula petals
- ½ tsp grated fresh ginger
- ½ tsp ground cinnamon
- ½ tsp orange peel (dried or fresh)
- 1 tsp honey (optional)
- A pinch of black pepper (to enhance turmeric absorption)

Instructions:

1. In a small pan, bring 1 cup of water to a gentle boil.
2. Add turmeric, calendula, ginger, cinnamon, orange peel, and black pepper (if using). Reduce heat and simmer for 5 minutes.
3. Remove from heat, cover, and let steep for another 5 minutes.
4. Strain into a cup, add honey if desired, and stir well.
5. Drink in the morning, or ahead of a creative task to awaken your inner fire.

Sun Blessing Oil

This infused oil channels solar radiance, encouraging joy, confidence, and protection. It can be used for anointing the solar plexus, as a massage oil, or in candle magic for success and vitality.

Ingredients:

- 1 tbsp dried St. John's wort
- 1 tsp dried orange peel
- 1 tsp dried ginger
- 1 cup carrier oil (olive, jojoba, or sunflower)
- 5 drops frankincense essential oil (optional)

Instructions:

1. Place St. John's wort, orange peel, and ginger in a clean glass jar.
2. Cover with carrier oil, ensuring all herbs are submerged.
3. Seal the jar and place it in a sunny spot for two to four weeks, shaking occasionally.
4. Strain and store in a dark bottle.
5. Use to anoint your wrists, solar plexus, or temples before important events to channel solar confidence.

Solar Radiance Incense

Burn this incense to invoke joy, creativity, and motivation. Ideal for morning rituals, manifestation work, or honoring the Sun in celestial observances.

Ingredients:

- 1 tsp dried orange peel
- 1 tsp dried calendula flowers
- 1 tsp crushed fresh ginger
- ½ tsp frankincense resin (for enhanced solar energy)
- ½ tsp ground cinnamon

Instructions:

1. Using a mortar and pestle, grind all ingredients into a fine powder.
2. Store in an airtight jar.
3. Burn on a charcoal disc while setting intentions for success and vitality.

The Moon: Balance and Intuition

Lunar Dream Tea

A brew that enhances dreams, intuition, and emotional flow. This gentle tea soothes the nervous system and encourages deep, symbolic dreaming.

Ingredients:

- 1 tsp dried mugwort
- 1 tsp dried chamomile
- ½ tsp white rose petals
- ½ tsp lemon balm (for calming effects)
- ½ tsp aniseed (for dream recall)
- 1 cup hot water

Instructions:

1. Place all herbs in a teapot or strainer.
2. Pour hot water over the herbs and steep for 7–10 minutes.
3. Strain and drink before bedtime, setting an intention to receive dream messages.

Full Moon Bath

A soothing bath to harmonize emotions and cleanse energy under the full moon. This herbal remedy is perfect for releasing stagnant emotions and aligning with the lunar cycle.

Ingredients:

- 1 cup Epsom salt
- ½ cup dried poppy petals
- ½ cup dried chamomile
- 5 drops rosemary essential oil
- 3 drops lavender essential oil

Instructions:

1. Using a spoon, mix the salts and dried herbs together in a bowl.
2. Add the essential oils and mix thoroughly.
3. Pour into a warm bath and soak, visualizing emotional renewal.

Moon Mist Spray

A mist that creates a calming, dreamy atmosphere. Ideal for use before meditation, sleep, or moon rituals.

Ingredients:

- ½ cup distilled water
- 10 drops white rose essential oil
- 5 drops chamomile essential oil
- 5 drops lavender essential oil
- 1 small clear quartz crystal (optional, for energetic infusion)

Instructions:

1. Combine all the ingredients in a spray bottle.
2. Shake the bottle well and allow the quartz crystal to infuse overnight under moonlight.
3. Spray around your space or onto pillows for a serene ambiance. Store for up to 6 months.

Crystals in water-based rituals:
While clear quartz crystals are considered water-safe, other may not be, so if you use a different crystal, it's always safer to use an indirect method: simply place the crystals next to the bottle overnight, under the moonlight, as submerging it for long periods may affect its durability and color. The crystal may also have unknown inclusions that may release toxic elements.

Mercury: Communication and Intellect

Mental Clarity Elixir

A stimulating tea that sharpens focus, enhances the memory, and supports mental agility.

Ingredients:

- 1 tsp dried brahmi
- 1 tsp dried ginkgo
- ½ tsp cardamom seeds
- ½ tsp lemon zest
- ½ tsp dried rosemary
- 1 cup hot water

Instructions:

1. Combine all the herbs in a teapot or infuser.
2. Pour hot water over the herbs and steep for 5-7 minutes.

Incense for Eloquence (Burning Ritual)

An energized incense to enhance communication and mental flow. Perfect for writers, speakers, and also students.

Ingredients:

- 1 tsp dried lavender
- 1 tsp crushed cardamom pods
- ½ tsp dried valerian root
- ½ tsp dried peppermint (for mental sharpness)

Instructions:

1. Using a mortar and pestle, grind all the ingredients into a powder.
2. Burn on a charcoal disc while setting communication-related intentions.
3. Strain and sip while studying, writing, or preparing for a presentation.

Throat Chakra Anointing Oil

A ritual oil to support self-expression and clarity in communication.

Ingredients:

- 1 tbsp almond oil
- 5 drops lavender essential oil
- 3 drops cardamom essential oil
- 2 drops peppermint essential oil
- A small blue stone (optional, for throat chakra activation)

Instructions:

1. Mix all the ingredients in a small glass bottle and allow it to sit overnight with the blue stone inside.
2. Use to anoint the throat chakra ahead of speaking engagements or creative work.

Venus: Love and Harmony

Love Sachet Talisman

A charm bag to attract love, romance, and positive relationships.

Ingredients:

- 3 dried rose petals
- 1 tsp dried vervain
- ½ tsp cinnamon chips (for attraction)
- 3 drops damiana tincture (optional)
- 1 small pink or red pouch

Instructions:

1. If using a tincture, drop it onto the herbs and allow them to dry slightly.
2. Place all the herbs in a pouch.
3. Carry the pouch, or place it under your pillow to promote enhanced love energy.

Aphrodite's Heart-Opening Tea

A floral infusion that enhances love, beauty, and emotional warmth. This tea nourishes the heart chakra and supports both self-love and harmony in relationships.

Ingredients:

- 1 tsp dried rose petals
- 1 tsp dried damiana
- ½ tsp dried vervain
- ½ tsp dried hibiscus (for attraction and beauty)
- ½ tsp cinnamon chips (for warmth and magnetism)
- 1 cup hot water
- 1 tsp raw honey (to sweeten the heart)

Instructions:

1. Combine all the herbs in a teapot or infuser.
2. Pour hot water over the herbs and steep for 7–10 minutes.
3. Strain and stir in the honey.
4. Sip slowly, focusing on self-love.

Beauty Bath

A luxurious ritual bath infused with Venusian energy to enhance self-love, attraction, and inner radiance.

Ingredients:

- ½ cup dried rose petals
- ¼ cup dried chamomile
- ½ cup Himalayan pink salt
- 5 drops rose essential oil
- 3 drops vanilla essential oil
- 1 small pink or rose quartz crystal (optional)

Instructions:

1. Using a spoon, mix the dried herbs, salt, and essential oils in a bowl.
2. Fill a warm bath and sprinkle the mixture into the water.
3. Soak while visualizing beauty and love radiating from within.

Mars: Action and Strength

Warrior's Power Tonic

An energizing tonic that ignites strength, courage, and stamina. A great remedy to take before workouts, high-energy tasks, or ahead of challenging situations.

Ingredients:

- 1 tsp dried nettle
- ½ tsp black pepper
- ½ tsp ground cinnamon
- ½ tsp dried basil
- ½ tsp grated fresh ginger
- 1 cup hot water
- 1 tsp honey

Instructions:

1. Combine all the herbs in a teapot.
2. Pour hot water over the herbs and steep for 5–7 minutes.
3. Strain and drink before any physically or mentally demanding activity.

Protection Incense (Burning Ritual)

An incense blend for strength, courage, and protection.

Ingredients:

- 1 tsp dried basil
- 1 tsp dried nettle
- ½ tsp crushed black peppercorns
- ½ tsp dragon's blood resin (optional, for added potency)

Instructions:

1. Grind all the ingredients into a fine powder using a mortar and pestle.
2. Store in an airtight jar (up to 6 months).
3. Burn a small amount on a charcoal disc to invoke Mars' protective energy.

Strength and Endurance Oil

An oil blend for resilience, confidence, and sustained energy.

Ingredients:

- 1 tbsp carrier oil (coconut, olive, or almond)
- 5 drops cinnamon essential oil
- 3 drops black pepper essential oil
- 2 drops clove essential oil

Instructions:

1. Mix all the ingredients together in a small bottle.
2. Anoint wrists, temples, and lower back before workouts or difficult tasks.

Jupiter: Expansion and Abundance

Violet Success Candle Ritual

A candle ritual for career advancement, knowledge, and personal growth.

Ingredients:

- 1 violet flower
- 1 gold or purple candle
- 3 drops saffron-infused oil

Instructions:

1. Place the violet flower beside the candle.
2. Using a sharp object such as a knife, carve your intention into the candle.
3. Anoint the candle with saffron oil and burn it while visualizing success.

Prosperity and Growth Elixir

A warming herbal tea to attract abundance, luck, and wisdom.

Ingredients:

- 1 tsp dried saffron
- ½ tsp crushed cloves
- ½ tsp dried daisy
- ½ tsp dried violet
- 1 cup hot water

Instructions:

1. Steep the herbs in hot water for 5 minutes.
2. Strain and drink while visualizing abundance and success flowing into your life.

Luck Bath

A prosperity bath to manifest wealth, opportunities, and success.

Ingredients:

- 1 cup elderflower cordial
- 1 tsp ground cinnamon
- ½ cup sea salt
- 5 drops bergamot essential oil

Instructions:

1. Add all the ingredients to warm bathwater and gently mix.
2. Soak for at least 15 minutes, focusing on expansion and abundance.

Saturn: Structure and Discipline

Banishing Oil

A protective oil to be used topically for setting firm boundaries.

Ingredients:

- 1 tbsp carrier oil (olive, jojoba, or sunflower)
- 5 drops cypress essential oil
- 3 drops black pepper essential oil

Instructions:

1. Combine all the oils in a glass jar.
2. Use to anoint doors, windows, or the body.

Grounding Tea

A stabilizing tea for focus, resilience, and patience.

Ingredients:

- 1 tsp dried barley
- ½ tsp dried arnica
- ½ tsp dried cypress
- 1 cup hot water

Instructions:

1. Combine all the herbs, then cover with hot water. Steep for 7 minutes.
2. Strain and drink when seeking clarity and stability.

Banishing Oil

A protective oil to be used topically for setting firm boundaries.

Ingredients:

- 1 tbsp carrier oil (olive, jojoba, or sunflower)
- 5 drops cypress essential oil
- 3 drops black pepper essential oil

Instructions:

1. Combine all the oils in a glass jar.
2. Use to anoint doors, windows, or the body.

Uranus: Innovation and Change

Breakthrough Brew

A stimulating tea for inspiration and original thinking.

Ingredients:

- 1 tsp dried and ground rhodiola
- ½ tsp dried and ground nutmeg
- 1 cup hot water

Instructions:

1. Combine the rhodiola and nutmeg, then add the hot water. Steep for 5 minutes.
2. Drink before brainstorming sessions or problem-solving.

Electric Mind Incense

An incense blend to enhance mental clarity, awaken higher insights, and support breakthroughs in creative and intellectual work. Ideal for use during brainstorming sessions, meditation, or problem-solving.

Ingredients:

- 1 tsp dried yarrow
- 1 tsp dried coffee beans
- ½ tsp crushed nutmeg
- ½ tsp frankincense resin
- ½ tsp dried peppermint

Instructions:

1. Grind all the ingredients into a fine powder using a mortar and pestle.
2. Store in an airtight jar (up to 6 months).
3. Burn a small amount on a charcoal disc before engaging in creative work, innovation, or spiritual exploration.

Mind-opening Anointing Oil

An anointing oil that encourages personal evolution, adaptability, and forward-thinking action. It helps to break through stagnation and opens the mind to new perspectives and bold ideas.

Ingredients:

- 1 tbsp carrier oil (jojoba, almond, or olive)
- 5 drops rhodiola essential oil
- 3 drops peppermint essential oil
- 3 drops nutmeg essential oil
- 1 small piece of clear quartz

Instructions:

1. Combine all the ingredients in a small glass bottle.
2. Shake the bottle well and allow to sit for one full Uranian cycle (seven days) in a bright, airy space to charge the blend.
3. Anoint your temples, third eye, or pulse points before engaging in projects, decision-making, or manifestation.

Neptune: Dreams and Spirituality

Veil Mist

A sacred mist which is perfect for deep meditation, divination, and connection to the subconscious.

Ingredients:

- ½ cup distilled water
- 10 drops blue lotus essential oil
- 5 drops lavender essential oil (for calm and intuition)
- 3 drops clary sage essential oil (for dream clarity and visioning)
- 1 small amethyst crystal (optional, to enhance Neptune's energy)

Instructions:

1. Combine all the ingredients in a glass spray bottle.
2. Shake the bottle well and allow the amethyst crystal to charge the blend overnight under moonlight.
3. Mist around your space or onto your pillow before sleep, meditation, or spiritual rituals.

Mystic Dream Elixir

A soothing brew that can be drunk to enhance dream recall and intuition.

Ingredients:

- 1 tsp dried blue lotus flowers
- ½ tsp dried passionflower
- ½ tsp dried wild lettuce
- 1 cup hot water

Instructions:

1. Combine all the ingredients, then cover with hot water. Steep for 7 minutes.
2. Strain and drink before meditation or sleep.

Oceanic Bath

A soothing and mystical bath inspired by Neptune's connection to the ocean, dreams, and intuition. This blend helps to cleanse energetic blockages, heightens psychic awareness, and enhances spiritual connection.

Ingredients:

- 1 cup sea salt
- ½ cup dried blue lotus flowers
- ½ cup dried marshmallow root
- 5 drops sandalwood essential oil
- 3 drops lavender essential oil

Instructions:

1. Using a spoon, mix the salt and dried herbs in a bowl.
2. Add the essential oils, mixing well.
3. Fill a warm bath and sprinkle the mixture into the water.
4. Soak for at least 20 minutes, while visualizing spiritual renewal and clarity washing over you.

Pluto: Transformation and Regeneration

Integration Herbal Balm

A balm for emotional and energetic renewal. This balm is grounding, protective, and helps to release negative and stagnant energy.

Ingredients:

- ½ cup olive oil (carrier)
- 1 tbsp dried black walnut leaves
- 1 tbsp dried skullcap
- ½ tbsp dried rosemary
- 1 tbsp beeswax
- 5 drops frankincense essential oil

Instructions:

1. In a double boiler, warm the olive oil and add the herbs. Simmer on a low heat for 20 minutes, allowing them to infuse.
2. Strain out the herbs and return the oil to the heat.
3. Add the beeswax and stir until it is fully melted.
4. Remove from the heat and stir in the essential oil.
5. Pour into a small jar and let cool before use.
6. Apply the balm to wrists, temples, or heart chakra before deep meditation.

Transformation Tea

A purifying tea for rebirth and gaining inner strength.

Ingredients:

- 1 tsp dried black walnut leaves
- ½ tsp dried skullcap
- ½ tsp dragon's blood resin
- 1 cup hot water

Instructions:

1. Combine all the ingredients, then cover with hot water. Steep for 7 minutes.
2. Strain and drink during times of transition and shadow work.

Smoke Cleanse

A burning ritual for energetic clearing and renewal, this cleanse allows you to release old patterns, break spiritual blockages, and mark the end of a transformation cycle.

Ingredients:

- 1 tsp dried rosemary
- 1 tsp dried black walnut leaves
- ½ tsp myrrh resin
- ½ tsp dragon's blood resin

Instructions:

1. Crush all the ingredients into a fine blend using a mortar and pestle.
2. Store in an airtight jar until use.
3. Burn a small amount on a charcoal disc, allowing the smoke to wash over your body and space, releasing stagnant energies.

Index